“”

the art of dialogue

the art of dialogue

Exploring personality differences for more effective communication

Carolyn Zeisset

CENTER FOR APPLICATIONS OF PSYCHOLOGICAL TYPE, INC.
2815 NW 13th St., Suite 401 ⋅ Gainesville, FL 32609

Published by
Center for Applications of Psychological Type, Inc.
2815 NW 13th Street, Suite 401
Gainesville FL 32609
352.375.0160
www.capt.org

Center for Applications of Psychological Type, Inc., CAPT, Looking at Type, and LAT are trademarks or registered trademarks of the Center for Applications of Psychological Type, Inc. in the United States and other countries.

Introduction to Type is a trademark or registered trademark of the Myers-Briggs Type Indicator Trust in the United States and other countries.

Myers-Briggs Type Indicator, Myers-Briggs, and MBTI are trademarks or registered trademarks of the Myers-Briggs Type Indicator Trust in the United States and other countries.

Library of Congress Cataloging-in-Publication Data

Zeisset, Carolyn, 1941-
    The art of dialogue: exploring personality differences for more effective communication / Carolyn Zeisset.
        p. cm.
    Includes bibliographical references and index.
    ISBN 0-935652-77-9
    ISBN 978-0935652-77-2
    1. Typology (Psychology) 2. Oral communication. I. Title.

    BF698.3.Z45 2005
    155.2'6--dc22

2005010143

To Tim, Michelle, Crista, and Heidi,
who lovingly teach me appreciation of differences
in psychological type and communication.

Table of Contents

Tables and Figures **xi**
Foreword **xiii**
Preface **xv**
Acknowledgments **xvii**

Communication and Psychological Type 1

chapter 1 **Contributions of Psychological Type to Communication 3**
What Is Psychological Type? **4**
    What Are Type Preferences? **5**
    The Eight Preferences **6**
The How and What of Communication **7**
Effective Communication **8**
    What If Another Person's Type Is Not Known? **9**
Type Identity Is Not Imposed **9**
A Word about This Book **9**
    A Comment about the Stories **10**

Personality Type Preferences and Function Pairs 11

chapter 2 **Extraversion and Introversion 13**
Extraversion and Introversion in Action **16**
Children and Type **23**
Communication That Works **24**

chapter 3 **Judging and Perceiving 27**
Judging and Perceiving in Action **28**
Children and Type **36**
Communication That Works **39**

chapter 4   **Sensing and Intuition 43**
Sensing and Intuition in Action 45
Children and Type 50
Communication That Works 51

chapter 5   **Thinking and Feeling 55**
Thinking and Feeling in Action 57
Children and Type 66
Communication That Works 68

chapter 6   **Focus on the Functions 71**
Getting the Communication Started 71
Function Pairs in Action 74
The Z Pattern 83
Children and Type 85
Communication That Works 87
Summing Up Use of Preferences and Function Pairs
    in Communication 88

Type Dynamics 91

chapter 7   **The Basics of Type Dynamics 93**
Premise of Type Dynamics Theory 93
    Whole Type 93
Two Basic Concepts of Type Dynamics 94
    Balance 95
    The Hierarchy of the Functions 96
The Role of Judging and Perceiving Preferences 100
Example of Type Dynamics 100
Order of Functions for Each Type 101

chapter 8   **Implications of Type Dynamics for Communication 103**
A Theory about Type and Communication 103
    Power of the Extraverted Dominant Function 104
    Extraverted Dominant Functions in Conflict 106
    Type Dynamics and Communication in Introverts 109
Research Studies 112
    A Note About Yeakley's Work 113

chapter 9 **Extraverted and Introverted Expressions of Functions 115**
Extraverted and Introverted Functions in Action 115
Effects of Unheard Functions 127

 Out-of-Pattern Communication 133

chapter 10 **Speaking from the Introverted Function 135**
Passion and the Introverted Function 135
  Signs of an Introverted Function Influenced by Passion 135
Introverted Dominant Function Speaks Out 136
Introverted Auxiliary Function Speaks Out 138
Stress and the Introverted Function 140

chapter 11 **Exaggerated Use of a Function 145**
Consequences of Overuse of a Function 145
Stress and Exaggerated Functions 146
Type Development and Exaggerated Functions 152

chapter 12 **Constructive Use of Differences 159**
Ineffective Adaptation to Type Preferences 160
Constructive Adaptation to Type Preferences 161
Principles for the Constructive Use of Type 163

 Language in Type and Communication 165

chapter 13 **Type and the Use of Language 167**
Same Words, Different Meanings 167
Different Words, Same Meaning 174
In Summary 175

chapter 14 **Talking about Type 177**
Avoiding Stereotypes 177
Avoiding Oversimplification 181
Upholding the Validity of Type Theory 184

chapter 15 **Suggestions for Further Investigation of Type and Communication 185**

Role of the Extraverted Function in Communication 185

Out-of-pattern Communication 186

Listening 187

Word Analysis 187

Gender Differences 188

References and Selected Bibliography 189

Index 191

Resources 195

tables and figures

table 2.1   Characteristics of Extraversion and Introversion 14

table 3.1   Characteristics of Judging and Perceiving 29

table 4.1   Characteristics of Sensing and Intuition 44

table 4.2   Suggestions for Teaching to People Preferring Sensing and Intuition 52

table 5.1   Characteristics of Thinking and Feeling 56

table 6.1   Characteristics of Function Pairs 76

table 7.1   Attitude of the Third Function 98

table 7.2   Order and Direction of Functions in Each Type 102

table 8.1   Order and Direction of Functions in Each Type 105

table 8.2   Order and Direction of Communication Functions in Each Type 105

table 9.1   Extraverted and Introverted Expressions of Functions 116

table 13.1   Suggestions for Listening to the Language of the Functions 175

figure 3.1   Outer Orientation 28

figure 6.1   ST Financial Statement 75

figure 6.2   NF Financial Statement 75

figure 6.3   Z Pattern: A Decision-Making Strategy 84

figure 8.1   Stretch of Communication Functions: Carolyn to Ray 110

figure 8.2   Stretch of Communication Functions: Ray to Carolyn 110

foreword

In *The Art of Dialogue*, Carolyn Zeisset has created a meticulously woven tapestry, rich in pattern and color, as she unfolds an effective methodology for increasing our skills and understanding in the art of communication through the perspective of individual personality differences. Her tool is the Myers-Briggs Type Indicator® (MBTI®) assessment based on the ideas of Carl G. Jung.

The patterns chosen make a unique contribution to the literature in that they encompass twenty-five years of progress by experienced MBTI practitioners in increasing the depth of understanding of Jungian psychological type. Each pattern reflects one more step in the expansion of this knowledge.

The colors are her treasury of stories, which illustrate the value of looking at communication through the lens of type. These stories, and her manner in presenting them, make the knowledge of type come alive and apply to daily life. Her approach is original and provides a key to new insights for the reader.

This reader has the sense that the author is focused on sharing her knowledge and experience in a language that is easily understandable to the lay person as well as the practitioner. She succeeds in using language that is simple and comprehensible without being simplistic.

The book is structured around the following steps for gaining in-depth understanding of psychological type: basic type preferences (Extraversion–Introversion, Sensing–Intuition, Thinking–Feeling, Judging–Perceiving); function pairs in the core of type (ST, SF, NF, NT); the eight Jungian processes that comprise the core of type in both extraverted and introverted expressions; type dynamics (the interaction of preferences) and the life-long development of type. Each section is illuminated by carefully selected stories.

The author has developed a rhythm that gives the reader a how-to method of using type perspective in understanding both the dynamics and ways of enhancing each communication exchange. The pattern throughout the book is content followed by examples of type in action through the use of stories; listening for type clues; and appropriate application of type to the situation. Each segment of theory is illustrated from Zeisset's treasury of stories with comments on the specific clues within the story that knowledge of type gives to understanding the communications. I found that this methodology improved the depth and sensitivity of my own perceptiveness. I will refer back to the examples often to refresh this skill and the insight I have gained.

Threads of gold woven throughout the tapestry provide further richness into nuances of type which lead to integrity of use. Among them: the author's list of what type is and what it is not; the importance of verification by the person involved; the implications of type dynamics on communication; the influence of passion and stress on communication; questions to be asked in problem solving. Do notice these bits of gold as you read.

Isabel Briggs Myers, creator of the MBTI assessment, was a pioneer in giving individuals access to knowing their personality type and making it useful in their lives. MBTI practitioners follow this tradition. Zeisset shares her insights and experiences, making them accessible to those who are new to type as well as to longtime practitioners.

One of the joys to this reader is the way Zeisset weaves the names and quotations from the work of leaders in this continuing movement into new territory through the tapestry of her book. To me, it showed a refreshing generosity of spirit and gave a sense of fellow travelers in this exploration.

There is a consistent theme in the career life of Carolyn Zeisset. The focus of her master's degree was individual differences followed by her work in teaching and curriculum development with a specialization in the education of gifted and developmentally challenged students. When introduced to the MBTI in 1981, she discovered an instrument and approach congruent with her own interest in "the constructive use of differences." She continued her work in applying type-identified learning styles to a learning center approach. At that time she started her collection of real life incidents illustrating the relationship between type and communication.

She and her husband, Ray, have spent these years fine tuning the Zeisset Associates Qualifying Program, perusing the literature, and participating in the MBTI community and its activities. Both as individuals and a team they have demonstrated a quiet and powerful presence that moves any activity forward.

This book is a carefully distilled culmination of all Carolyn Zeisset has observed and accomplished. It gives people a how-to model of using psychological type and the MBTI soundly, helpfully, respectfully, and above all, with integrity. The reader can trust the information both in content and attitude whether it is used for personal development or with clients.

Katharine D. Myers, Trustee,
Myers-Briggs Type Indicator Trust, April 2005

the art of dialogue

preface

The workshop topic was psychological type. The schedule called for brief introductions to several applications. The first application was psychological type and communication.

During a break, a workshop participant approached me with an apology. He had become so engrossed in thinking about implications of type in his communications with his secretary that he had tuned out the rest of the presentation. Lost in his own thoughts, he recognized sources of confusion in discussions with his secretary and saw ways that he could reword his requests to make them clearer and more understandable.

Communication is integral to relationships, whether business or personal, casual or intimate, short-term or ongoing. Perhaps this relevance explains why the communication application often sparks the greatest interest in workshops on psychological type.

Communication is also a window into our own psychological type and the type of others. I frequently hear myself saying something in a way that reflects my own personality type. Similarly, by listening carefully to others, I can often get clues to their possible types, or at least to the preferences from which they are speaking at a particular moment.

This book is a result of more than twenty years of listening to others and collecting stories about the interaction of psychological type and communication. Although communication is both written and spoken, the primary focus of this book is oral communication.

The book begins with an introduction to psychological type and to communication. Four sections follow this introduction: one about type preferences and function pairs, one about type dynamics, one about out-of-pattern communication, and one about the use of language.

As you read this book, you may recognize your own expressions of type in everyday activities and in interactions with others. You may find an aha, an understanding that until now has eluded you. You may find a suggestion to try. At the very least, I hope you find one or more stories that resonate with your experience or that you simply enjoy reading.

acknowledgments

The stories in this book are selected from a collection that I began in 1981 when I first started learning about psychological type. I thank family, friends, co-workers, and countless participants in type workshops and training sessions for their contributions to this growing collection of stories.

Through the years many individuals in the type community have contributed to my ever-increasing knowledge of type. Those who especially come to mind include John DiTiberio, Sandra Hirsh, Linda Kirby, Otto Kroeger, Jean Kummerow, Gordon Lawrence, Mary McCaulley, Katharine D. Myers, and Naomi Quenk.

Flavil Yeakley introduced me to the application of type and communication. Through the years that I have conducted training with the Myers-Briggs Type Indicator® (MBTI®) instrument, participants have found the insights I learned from him to be a high point of the training.

I also want to express gratitude to Markey Read and Ellie Sommer. Markey is a friend and co-trainer who keeps me aware of the many expressions of type dynamics. Ellie, editorial director at the Center for Applications of Psychological Type, has offered valuable editorial suggestions. To the many unnamed others who have also been my teachers, I offer my thanks.

My greatest thanks go to my husband, Ray, for forty-five years of friendship and love, for twenty-five years of help as a co-trainer, for seven years of support during this writing project, and for countless hours of attention to the details of typing, formatting, and editing which otherwise might not have received such a high priority.

part one communication and psychological type

Communication is a basic activity of our lives. We expend energy and time every day trying to connect with others through words. Communication is integral to relationships.

Psychological type influences all of communication—what we say, what we hear, what we want to hear. This book explores the interaction of communication and psychological type.

Knowing what psychological type is, as well as what it is not, helps us use type to enhance communication. Psychological type preferences help us understand both the how and the what of communication. Recognizing our own role in communication contributes to the effective use of type in communication. Part 1 of this book describes the basic aspects of psychological type and how they affect communication.

"Type concepts are useful whenever one person must communicate with another or live with another or make decisions that affect another's life."

Isabel Briggs Myers, *Gifts Differing*

chapter 1 contributions of psychological type to communication

Communication is key to satisfaction in any situation in which two or more people relate to each other. When asked what is needed for effective relationships or work settings, people are likely to say good communication.

Most people are aware that lack of communication is a common source of frustration, tension, stress, and strained or broken relationships. Sometimes communication fails because individuals do not put forth the effort required for effective communication, but sometimes people do invest great effort, and still communication fails. During communication, messages such as these fly past people into some unknown space:

"If you'd just say what you mean."

"I told you. Why don't you listen?"

"You don't understand."

In such cases, the truth just might be that one person did say what that individual meant, and the other person did listen. Still, the two did not understand each other.

Communication is complex, with many factors contributing to the success or breakdown of understanding. One major factor is that the definition of *good communication* differs from one person to another. Information that one person wants or needs is different from the information that another person wants or needs. What one individual considers most important may seem trivial to another. Preferred methods of communication also differ.

If wants, needs, and methods vary from one person to another, how can a person hope to establish effective communication? Fortunately, identifiable patterns and observable clues to communication preferences exist. The patterns relate to natural differences in personality.

A person who is aware of psychological type preferences can observe clues and adjust communication based on these observations. When even one person uses type preferences to help communicate, all individuals involved benefit. In such cases, people agree that effective listening and presentation of information and sound decision making have occurred. They usually have a sense of effective listening, exchange of information, and sound decision making. In addition, they experience mutual respect.

What Is Psychological Type?

Psychological type is a theory about personality preferences developed by the Swiss physician-psychologist Carl G. Jung and further described by the mother-daughter team of Katharine Cook Briggs and Isabel Briggs Myers. All three were interested in understanding people. Myers sought to bring to others an understanding of valuable differences, appreciation of one's own strengths and gifts, and recognition of potential areas for growth and development. She created a self-report questionnaire, the Myers-Briggs Type Indicator® (MBTI®) instrument, which helps people identify typical, natural, and enduring patterns of preferences in four areas:

- the preferred direction of energy and attention,
- the preferred way to take in information,
- the preferred way to make decisions, and
- the preferred lifestyle in the outer world.

These areas are described and illustrated in chapters 2 through 5 of this book.

Reading the descriptions included here can help you think about your own preferences and about different but valuable preferences of others. This endeavor is not a substitute for taking the MBTI instrument and receiving an interpretation from a qualified professional (see Resources, page 195). However, understanding type and preferences as presented in this book can lead to more constructive relationships and communication, thus moving you toward Isabel Myers's goal of the "constructive use of differences."

4

As you begin to learn about psychological type, it is important to become aware of what it is as well as what it is not. The two lists that follow highlight some key points to keep in mind.

Psychological type is
- an affirming way to understand yourself and others;
- a way to identify typical, natural, and enduring patterns of preferences; the theory assumes that type preferences are innate;
- a way to value the constructive use of differences;
- a way to strengthen relationships and improve communication; and
- a dynamic, not static, description of paths for interaction, adaptation, growth, and development.

Psychological type is NOT
- a way to pigeonhole, label, diagnose, prescribe, or excuse behavior. In psychological type
  - each person verifies his or her own preferences;
  - people of the same type have many characteristics in common but also have individual expressions of characteristics;
  - each person uses preferences that are less preferred as they are needed but relies on those that are preferred whenever possible; and
  - a person expresses preferences most easily and often in situations when the individual truly has a choice.
- a description of everything about human behavior. Human behavior is complex and cannot be described by any one framework or theoretical model.
- a way to determine skill, maturity, or development; psychological type only describes preferences; it does not tell how well a person uses those preferences.

What Are Type Preferences?

Psychological type is based on a theory that each of us has typical, natural, and innate patterns of preferences for how we use our minds. To understand the concept of preferences, try this exercise.
- Write your name.
- Put the pen or pencil in your other hand and write your name again.

Most people describe the first experience as comfortable, natural, and easy. It requires little or no thought. Most people describe the second experience with such terms as *awkward, unnatural, hard,* and *slow.* It requires concentration. Some people need to think about which way to turn the paper. Use of the less-preferred hand in the second exercise often results in a poor quality of handwriting, perhaps resembling that of a young child. Although people sometimes see writing with the less-preferred hand as an interesting challenge, they quickly say they would be frustrated and drained of energy if they had to take notes in a lecture class this way. They believe they would lose interest and might even give up the effort entirely.

Although we can and do use both hands for a variety of activities, we have a natural preference for using one hand more than the other, as the writing exercises demonstrate.

Psychological type preferences are like handedness preferences. Both are so natural that we tend not to notice them. The theory of psychological type assumes that type preferences are inborn.

When you communicate with another person, you use your natural preferences. You give or ask for the kind of information that is of primary interest to you. You make decisions in your preferred way, at your own pace.

If the person with whom you want to communicate has preferences different from yours, that person may stay engaged with you for a while. Over time the person may become frustrated, feel drained of energy, lose interest, and eventually tune you out completely. Understanding psychological type preferences can help you recognize such frustrations in others and help you make adaptations in your communication approach so that you do not require others to "write continually with the less-preferred hand."

The Eight Preferences

The MBTI instrument is based on a theory of psychological type that identifies eight patterns of mental behaviors. These eight patterns form the following four pairs of opposite preferences.

- Extraversion–Introversion
- Sensing–Intuition
- Thinking–Feeling
- Judging–Perceiving

Each person prefers one alternative to the other within each pair. A person's MBTI type is made up of four preferences, each represented by a letter (E or I,

S or N, T or F, J or P). All possible combinations of the eight preferences give sixteen psychological types.

For example, my own type code is INFP. My preference between Extraversion and Introversion is for Introversion (I). Between Sensing and Intuition, I have a preference for Intuition (N). I prefer Feeling (F) from the Thinking–Feeling alternatives and Perceiving (P) from the Judging–Perceiving alternatives. When I state my preferences to others, I tell them that my type is INFP.

The How and What of Communication

Psychological type preferences help us understand the how and what of communication.

Two of the four dichotomies just identified, Extraversion–Introversion and Judging–Perceiving, are the *how* of psychological type. They are called *attitudes* or orientations. (Some people use the term *attitude* for the Extraversion–Introversion dichotomy and the term *orientation* for the Judging–Perceiving dichotomy.) Attitudes or orientations impact the direction and use of the functions.

Attitude/orientation	Extraversion–Introversion	How
Perception function	Sensing–Intuition	What
Judgment function	Thinking–Feeling	What
Attitude/orientation	Judging–Perceiving	How

In communication, Extraversion–Introversion and Judging–Perceiving identify how a person prefers to receive or give a message. More detailed descriptions of attitudes or orientations are provided in chapters 2 and 3.

Two dichotomies, Sensing–Intuition and Thinking–Feeling, are the *what* part of psychological type. They are called functions and are the core of type, reflecting the following two fundamental processes:

- perception (gathering information through use of the Sensing or Intuition preference);
- judgment (making decisions or coming to conclusions about the information through use of the Thinking or Feeling preference).

Note that the terms perception and judgment just used here name the fundamental mental processes of information gathering and decision making—the former referring to Sensing-Intuition and the latter to Thinking–Feeling preferences. As we saw in the previous discussion of attitudes and orientations, the terms Judging and Perceiving also name two preferences. Just as a dictionary entry may include two different definitions of a word, so type language includes two uses of the terms perception and judgment or Judging and Perceiving. The two uses of the terms are related, and this relationship is described in chapter 3.

In communication the content of messages comes through the perception functions of Sensing and Intuition and the judgment functions of Thinking and Feeling. More detailed descriptions of the functions appear in chapters 4 and 5.

Effective Communication

There are two general rules for effective communication.

- It is the responsibility of the sender of a message to adapt to the receiver's communication mode.
- It is the responsibility of the person who understands psychological type (whether that person is the sender or the receiver) to adapt to the communication mode of the person who does not know type.

However, when the following conditions exist, it is not necessary to adapt communication:

- Dialogue occurs.
- Both parties are tuned in and engaged.
- Each party feels that the other listens and hears.
- The needs of each are met for discussion and reflection, for pacing, for getting information and reaching decisions, and for structure and flexibility.

As Kummerow, Barger, and Kirby (1997) note in *WorkTypes*, "If your style works for you and doesn't impact others negatively, keep it."

Communication that meets these conditions does not generally get a lot of press, but such communication can and does occur among people of all psychological types. When someone says, "Somehow, we just clicked," effective communication has taken place.

However, the common experience for most people is that communication does not just *click*. Individuals need to make adaptations for effective communication to occur.

What If Another Person's Type Is Not Known?

In most situations, an individual cannot verify another person's type prefer- ences. Yet, the communication is likely to be most effective if the speaker adapts to the other person's type. Just what do you do?

A good method for attempting to identify an individual's type preferences comes from basic scientific practices:

- Observe. Watch for possible clues about type.
- Form a hypothesis about one or more preferences.
- Test the hypothesis. Adjust your communication approach based on your hypothesis about preferences and observe the results.
- If careful observation suggests that effective communication is taking place, continue your approach.
- If the hypothesis does not work and you sense a communication gap, continue to observe, and form and test a new hypothesis.

In short-term interactions, adjusting language to match observable behaviors is often sufficient to establish communication for that particular situation, whether or not your hypothesis about the person's type is correct. In long-term relationships, the closer a person can come to identifying underly- ing type preferences, the more likely that person is to establish good communication and even to recognize patterns of communication that do not meet expectations, such as those described later in this book.

Type Identity Is Not Imposed

It is important to remember that an observer can only make a best guess about another person's type. An observer cannot impose a type identity on someone else. Only the individuals themselves can verify their own type. Verification of type involves understanding the theory of psychological type and knowing one- self well enough to be aware of patterns of mental behaviors that are typical for oneself.

A Word about This Book

In this book, lists of the characteristics of type preferences provide a beginning point for observation of personality type. Stories offer practical examples of type preferences in action.

Following each story is a section that identifies type clues revealed through careful listening. Some clues come directly from what people say and others from what they don't say. Some clues come from knowledge of the other person's interests and skills or observation of body language. No matter the source, these clues help formulate a hypothesis about a person's type. Further information for applying type follows some stories.

A Comment about the Stories

Some stories in the book are intact examples that are representative of similar stories. Others are compilations of bits of several stories. All names used in the stories have been changed, as have the details of some settings. At times, the dialogue has been edited for clarity. However, the substantive content and type characteristics of the communication remain unchanged.

Some readers may question whether dialogue is contrived to fit theory. The process I put in place was to report the dialogue and then analyze it according to theory.

In general, I hope that the stories in this book will be a tool to help readers identify how and where they can use psychological type to enhance communication. Through careful listening to your own stories, you will make surprising discoveries and gain rich insights into how psychological type affects your daily interactions and personal and professional relationships.

part two personality type preferences and function pairs

Understanding the eight preferences of psychological type is a first level of understanding communication. Paul Tieger and Barbara Barron-Tieger (2000) in their book *Just Your Type* report results of studies of personality type and relationship satisfaction. They interviewed therapists to identify key issues, surveyed 2,500 individuals, collected an extended questionnaire from 750 individuals, and conducted in-depth interviews with hundreds of couples, who represented all possible combinations of the sixteen personality types. Findings showed that effective communication was the most important aspect of a satisfying relationship for 92 percent of couples. Additionally, the more type preferences a couple had in common, the higher they rated satisfaction with communication.

Part 2 of this book focuses on the eight preferences. It includes five chapters, one on each of the four dichotomies and one on combinations of the functions Sensing, Intuition, Thinking, and Feeling. Each chapter includes stories that show type preferences in action, along with sections that describe clues to psychological type and its application.

"Whenever people differ, a knowledge of type
helps to cut out irrelevant friction. More than that, it
points up the advantages of the differences."

Gordon Lawrence, *People Types and Tiger Stripes*

chapter 2 extraversion and introversion

Extraversion and Introversion identify *how* a person prefers to receive or give a message. They show the direction of a person's energy and attention. Extraversion and Introversion are the opposite preferences in the first dichotomy. A person's preference on this dichotomy shows up as the first letter in a psychological type code (E or I).

Attitude/Orientation	Extraversion–Introversion	How
Perception function	Sensing–Intuition	What
Judgment function	Thinking–Feeling	What
Attitude/orientation	Judging–Perceiving	How

Extraversion (always spelled with an a) means "outward turning." People who prefer Extraversion tend to be energized by and turn their attention to people, activity, and things around them. *Introversion* means "inward turning." People who prefer Introversion tend to be energized by and turn their attention to their inner world of ideas, memories, reactions, or images.

As with handedness, we can and do use both Extraversion and Introversion, but we have a natural preference for one of these alternatives over the other. Table 2.1 (pages 14–15) lists characteristics of people who prefer Extraversion and those who prefer Introversion.

table 2.1
Characteristics of Extraversion and Introversion

People Who Prefer Extraversion	People Who Prefer Introversion
Tend to want others to know they	**Tend to want others to know they**
• are likely to come to know what they think about something by thinking out loud, hearing themselves say it, bouncing ideas off others and responding to their reactions, building on the ideas of others. To Introverts this looks as if they are always changing their minds	• are likely to come to know what they think about something by reflecting silently, holding conversations inside their head between themselves and the other parties involved, and speaking only after internal thought. To Extraverts this looks as if they expect others to read their minds
In communication, tend to	**In communication, tend to**
• express themselves freely • offer opinions readily, share experiences, and advocate for their own ideas and needs • want to be included in all communication, even spur-of-the-moment discussion	• observe and reflect before speaking • wait to be asked before speaking or giving an opinion • want advance notice of topics of discussion
In interpersonal relationships, may	**In interpersonal relationships, may**
• greet people easily • welcome people stopping by • engage and involve others in conversations • work in groups • see meetings as places for group work • network	• wait for others to greet them • experience people stopping by or phoning as interruptions • stay in the background • work alone or with one or two others behind the scenes • see meetings as interruptions to work or situations where more work is created • have fewer but more intense relationships

the art of dialogue

table 2.1 *continued*
Characteristics of Extraversion and Introversion

People Who Prefer Extraversion	People Who Prefer Introversion
Often prefer to learn through	**Often prefer to learn through**
• discussions, asking questions • talking to others about their experiences • knowing what others expect of them • knowing a little bit about a lot of areas of interest	• listening, reading, and pondering • one-on-one conversations, writing, and solving problems on their own • setting own standards • knowing in depth about a few areas of interest
Others often observe that they may	**Others often observe that they may**
• speak rapidly and loudly • make immediate eye contact • be more animated • go to others • have a short attention span • interrupt • interpret a general statement in the context of a specific situation • like to be involved in activities and make events happen, not just think about them • move quickly to action	• speak slowly and quietly, often pausing before speaking and while speaking • avoid eye contact • be reserved • stay in own space • be able to concentrate for long periods of time • not interrupt even when it would be appropriate • interpret a statement in the context of a key word or phrase in the statement • like the idea or plan for something better than actually doing it • want to formulate a clear idea of what to do before moving to action
Others may be put off because they	**Others may be put off because they**
• often initially energize others, but then may dominate conversations and overwhelm others, Extraverts as well as Introverts • may neglect to listen to responses of others, responding more to what they hear themselves say as they clarify their thoughts	• often appear as uninvolved, though they are actively listening and reflecting • may neglect to say aloud what they have said to themselves inside their head, though they often believe they have spoken their thoughts aloud

Extraversion and Introversion in Action

The stories that follow are examples of Extraversion and Introversion in action. Read each story as if you were overhearing a bit of ordinary, everyday conversation. Remember that in such a setting, you are unlikely to have a placard or answer key that announces the speaker's type code. However, as you listen to each speaker, you may hear possible type-related clues. You may hear clues in the choice of subject matter, the specific words used, the sentence structure, or the speaker's viewpoint.

Diane and Dave: How Do We Communicate?

Diane and Dave work in the same company. They have different perspectives about how to communicate with each other and with the public. As you hear each tell about the same situation, listen for clues that may lead you to a hypothesis about the type preference of each on the Extraversion and Introversion dichotomy.

> **Diane:** I can't seem to get Dave to communicate. At our petroleum company we have periodic interdepartmental meetings. I'm the public relations coordinator, and I get ideas for news releases from most departments during those meetings, but Dave seldom speaks at all. I've tried everything I can think of.
>
> The other day someone told me about some neat work Dave is doing, and right away I thought, that could make a good press release so I called him, but he didn't return my call, so I went over to the chemical engineering lab, but he acted like I shouldn't be there. It's not as if I don't know about a lab. I don't know everything about the petroleum business, but I have a degree in chemistry, and I was working in chemical engineering at another company before I heard about this job.
>
> A couple of days later Dave sent me a memo. It took me a while to get up the courage to open the envelope. My first thought was that I must have done something terribly wrong. Why else would someone write a memo? Why wouldn't he just pick up the phone or come and talk with me? The memo turned out to have some good information, but it was full of numbers and technical jargon. Sure, I can read it, but that's not going to make a story that will be interesting to people. Still, I feel awfully uneasy about rewriting it. He might send another memo. I don't understand why we can't just talk.

Dave: As chief chemical engineer at the petroleum company, I am required to attend interdepartmental meetings every two weeks. The meetings are a waste of time. The head of each department is supposed to report what is new. Chemical engineering is not a department with breaking news. I developed research protocols and a staff structure that work well, but it takes time to follow them. Generally, I don't have anything to report.

Three months ago corporate management hired a public relations officer. Diane was assigned to get press releases from all departments. She barged right into the lab and started asking questions. I wouldn't talk off the top of my head. The department has a reputation for careful, responsible work. If I answered questions on the spur of the moment, I might not say something right, but that would be what would be quoted.

I interrupted work I needed to do and put together the best data I could. I rewrote it three times. It took four and a half hours over the next two days. Then she didn't use it.

LISTENING FOR TYPE CLUES. Diane and Dave describe the same situation from different perspectives. An analysis of their stories reveals clues about the psychological type preferences shown by each.

Diane is comfortable with oral communication. She finds meetings to be places to network with others, share ideas and experiences, and get work done. When she has an idea or question, her first response is to talk with someone by phone or face-to-face. As she speaks, her thoughts tumble out one after the other. She assumes that space, particularly company space, is common territory. These are characteristics associated with a preference for Extraversion.

Dave is uncomfortable with oral communication. He sees meetings as interruptions to work time and as events where additional work is generated or assigned. He also sees phone calls and unplanned visits as interruptions. When he is asked a question, his first response is hesitation, as he wants to think about the issue before answering. He sees space, even a lab in a workplace, as private territory. These are characteristics associated with a preference for Introversion.

APPLYING TYPE: *Oral and written communication.* People who prefer Extraversion often report a negative first reaction to receiving memos. They sometimes say that they would write a memo or letter only for something very important or for news too bad to tell in person. Most communication for them is oral. They may express frustration at receiving e-mail from someone whose desk is only a few cubicles away.

People who prefer Introversion are likely to hesitate or have a negative first reaction to a spontaneous idea or question. They are often uncomfortable verbalizing an idea and then having to correct statements that they think might be misunderstood. They are uneasy about the possibility of sounding as if they are changing their minds. People who prefer Introversion are likely to prefer written communication so that they can reflect on the content of the communication and hone the precision of their own words.

LaKeisha and Jamal: Aircraft Carrier and Airport Runway

LaKeisha (ENFJ) describes her communication relationship with Jamal (INFJ) this way: When we're talking together, it's easy to see that Jamal and I are very different. Jamal is a slow responder. I'm like a plane on an aircraft carrier—I just take off and go. Jamal is more like a land-based plane. He has to back away from the terminal, taxi out to the runway, and wait for the runway to be clear before he takes off. Someone gave me another analogy that helps me to be patient. He said to think about when I turn on the computer, and the hourglass pops up. It doesn't do any good to bang on the computer or be in a hurry! You just have to wait until the hourglass turns into an arrow.

LISTENING FOR TYPE CLUES. LaKeisha, who has a preference for Extraversion, describes her method of communication as "just take off and go." People who prefer Extraversion tend to express themselves freely. They tend to respond more quickly and to speak more rapidly than do Introverts. LaKeisha describes Jamal as a slow responder. She implies that he speaks more slowly and is more reserved in his responses than she is. The characteristics LaKeisha describes for Jamal are associated with a preference for Introversion.

APPLYING TYPE: *Recognizing typical patterns.* To identify type preferences, we need to know ourselves well enough that we are aware of typical patterns in our mental behaviors. As we hear LaKeisha speak, we sense that she is aware of her own typical patterns of communication and her usual responses to Jamal's typical patterns. Such self-knowledge is an important part of identifying type preferences.

18   the art of dialogue

Greg and Charles: Who Talks?

Greg (ENTP) and Charles (INFJ) both teach at a local college. Their different teaching methods are expressions of their different preferences on the Extraversion–Introversion dichotomy.

> **Greg:** My primary method of instruction is the seminar. Before each class I announce a topic and suggest readings. The students are free to bring what they find from other resources. The discussions are stimulating and challenging. Sometimes a student asks a question that really makes me think or do further study. I think students learn best when they are their own teachers. I know I learn a lot from them.

> **Charles:** There is so much material we need to cover in this course that I have to plan carefully for each class. I outline all my lectures, and often write much of what I want to say. It's hard to say things clearly so they won't be misunderstood. Some of the students think we should have more discussion, but we seldom have that much time. When I have tried it, the students come up with crazy ideas or questions that aren't related to that day's topic. That doesn't seem like learning to me.

LISTENING FOR TYPE CLUES. Greg, who has a preference for Extraversion, is comfortable with the give and take of discussion. He finds it stimulating to think on his feet and interesting to look at the breadth of a topic.

Charles, who has a preference for Introversion, needs reflection and preparation time before he speaks. He is uncomfortable if he says something off the top of his head and then has to correct himself. He is most interested in the depth of the topic.

APPLYING TYPE: *Direction of energy.* Sometimes people assume that a person who talks a lot in a given situation must be an Extravert. For example, they assume that an instructor who lectures for an entire class period prefers Extraversion because the instructor talks the whole time. However, lecturing may be a comfortable teaching method for an Introvert because it allows the instructor to prepare ahead of time and avoid the uncomfortable position of having to think on one's feet.

As stated earlier, Extraversion and Introversion have to do with the preferred direction of energy and attention. A person who prefers Extraversion draws energy from the outer world of people and activities and things. A person who prefers Introversion draws energy from the inner world of thoughts, ideas, memories, and reflections.

Heath and Caralee: Talk Now/Talk Later

Heath has preferences for ENTP. His girlfriend Caralee has preferences for ISTJ. Differences in their communication patterns are particularly evident when they discuss a problem.

> **Heath:** My biggest problem with Caralee is that she has no communication skills. When we have an issue, I say the best way to get through it is to talk about it, but we just get started, and she clams up. We've only talked maybe half an hour, and I'm just starting to get an idea of what the issue really is, and she tunes out. If we could just keep talking, we could resolve the problem.

> **Caralee:** I like Heath, but sometimes he wears me out. I came home from work. As soon as I walked in the door, he said we had an issue. He didn't say what the issue was or ask when we could talk about it. He just started talking right then, and he went on and on. I asked, "What's your point?" and he said, "I'm getting to that." But, he didn't. I told him, "If you can't get to the point in fifteen minutes, we need to walk away and think about it. If a discussion goes more than half an hour, I'm so exhausted, I can't hear what you say, and I'm not responsible for anything I say."

LISTENING FOR TYPE CLUES. Heath, who has a preference for Extraversion, is ready to discuss an idea as soon as it comes to him. He figures out what he thinks as he hears his own words out loud. He needs responses from Caralee to build and refine his ideas, and a half hour is not long enough for a full discussion. In fact, for him, half an hour is a short amount of time.

Caralee, who has a preference for Introversion, needs transition time and advance notice in order to turn her attention to a topic of conversation. Interaction through discussion requires extra energy for Introverts. If Caralee has had to expend her energy in interactions at work, she is likely to be exhausted when she arrives home. She does not have energy at that point to enter a new discussion. In addition, she needs to know what the topic of conversation is

the art of dialogue

before she begins a discussion. She figures out what she thinks about the topic by reflecting on it, then talking, then reflecting again.

For Caralee, half an hour is a long time and goes beyond the time of a productive discussion, particularly if she has not had time in advance to formulate her thoughts. If a problem is too complex to resolve within a few minutes, she wants to intersperse discussion with reflection. She prefers to think about pieces of the problem one at a time.

APPLYING TYPE: *Clarifying thoughts.* Extraverts sometimes say, "I didn't know I thought that until I heard myself say it." Introverts sometimes report, "I wasn't clear in my own mind what I thought about that until later," or "I had to write it down and read what I wrote before I knew what I thought about that."

APPLYING TYPE: *Recharging the Introversion battery.* Introverts whose jobs require them to interact with others for most of the day need time to recharge their batteries before turning attention to interactions at home. Recharge time does not necessarily need to be long. Fifteen to thirty minutes may be sufficient. For some Introverts, the first thing they do when they come home from work is spend some time alone. They may read a newspaper, go to a garden, or walk the dog. Others see commuting as a way to get some reflection time. After that quiet time, people who prefer Introversion are ready for conversation.

Annette and Lois: Alone Time and Interaction Time

Annette has preferences for ESFP. Lois has preferences for INFP. Both have times for quiet and for interaction.

> **Annette:** My favorite time of day is the early morning when I go to my meditation garden with a book of readings, like one that gives you a thought for the day. The garden is so quiet and peaceful. My family knows to leave me alone when I'm there, unless it's an emergency. We're an active family—with work, school, and sports. We enjoy frequent and often spontaneous get-togethers with our extended families and friends. I love all these people and activities, but I also like my quiet time in my meditation garden—even though sometimes I invite some member of my family to come with me.

Lois: I'm a teacher in a new creative arts magnet school. Because of the nature of the school and students, we teachers develop a lot of our own curriculum. I thought I would write materials in the summer to use when school started, but every time I sat down to work, I just stared at the blank paper. I couldn't get started. I missed having other teachers to talk with. Now that school has started, I stay up late at night working out the ideas I get in discussions with teachers and students during the day.

APPLYING TYPE: *Alone time and interaction time.* A common misunderstanding about personality types is that a person like Annette, who expresses a desire for alone time, has a preference for Introversion. However, Extraverts also need some quiet or alone time.

Likewise, a common misunderstanding is that a person like Lois, who has a preference for Introversion, does not need or want interaction with others. People who have a preference for Introversion often report that they talk with others a few minutes to jumpstart their thinking. Then, they go off by themselves to reflect on the ideas or data.

APPLYING TYPE: *Adapting to the communication mode.* In a typical casual conversation, it is not always possible for a person who listens for type clues to know the psychological type of the speaker. Susan Brock (1991) notes that it is possible though to identify the mode of communication that a person is using at a particular moment.

The communication mode refers to type characteristics an individual expresses in a particular situation, whether or not those are the characteristics of the person's type preference. We remember that full use of type includes reliance on a person's preference, and appropriate use of the opposite alternative as it is needed.

In an initial, short-term interaction, a listener may not know whether the speaker is expressing the type preference or momentarily using the opposite alternative. For example, if I want to buy a new car, I am likely to begin the search using my preference for Introversion. I might read information about makes and models and perhaps browse in a dealer showroom. There comes a time, however, when I have formulated my questions. This may be the point when I am ready to meet a salesperson. The salesperson may assume that I am an Extravert because I want to actively talk through my questions. I would be miffed if the salesperson were to respond to my questions by handing me a brochure to read. At that point, I am communicating from an Extraversion mode rather than from my preference for Introversion.

If we were to observe Annette and Lois only in passing, we might assume that Annette has a preference for Introversion and Lois, a preference for Extraversion. Annette speaks about her quiet reflection time from an Introverted mode. She speaks about reading alone and being quiet. When Lois speaks about getting started with writing, she speaks of characteristics associated with Extraversion, such as a need for talking out ideas with others. Each indicates that the described activity lasts only a short time and is not the pattern for most of the day. For that brief time, however, each speaks in the mode of the opposite preference.

In short-term interactions, it can be sufficient to adapt to the momentary mode of communication, continue listening for type clues, and adapt again as the other person changes modes. In longer-term and more in-depth relationships, it is helpful to listen for clues to type preferences. In these relationships, communication is usually more effective if you speak most of the time to a person's preferences and recognize when the person momentarily changes modes.

Children and Type

Psychological type theorists think that Extraversion and Introversion may be the first preferences that are observable in children. Hints of such preferences can be seen in the interactions of Lissie and Garth with their adult neighbor.

Lissie and Garth

Lissie, age five, and Garth, age four, are playing in the front yard of their home. Thurmond, a retired neighbor, is taking his daily walk.

> Thurmond: Good morning. How are you today?
> (Lissie eyes Thurmond, leaves her toys, and backs toward the house where her mother is weeding a flower bed.)
>
> Garth: Want to see my new race car? I'll show you what it can do. My dad got it for me. See? It can go fast. Vroom. Vroom.

 LISTENING FOR TYPE CLUES. We would not want to leap to conclusions about the psychological types of Lissie and Garth for two reasons. One, they are very young and type development is a lifelong process and, two, we have had only one brief interaction with them. Still, we get hints that if we were to observe Lissie and Garth over a period of time, we might see patterns for Introversion in Lissie and for Extraversion in Garth. Lissie is unsure about interacting with the neighbor while Garth readily engages in conversation.

APPLYING TYPE: *Parenting a child with an Extraversion or Introversion preference.* Elizabeth Murphy (1992) in *The Developing Child* offers this suggestion for an Introverted parent of an Extraverted child: teach your child to say your name, count to ten silently inside his head, say your name again, and then tell you what he wants to say. This gives the parent time to pause in her own thoughts and turn attention to the child so that the parent can really listen to the child.

Murphy notes that sometimes when a parent attempts to teach social skills to an Introverted child, the parent asks the child many questions. The parent may try to force interaction with others by saying, "Tell about . . . " or "Say what you think about . . . " If the child answers, "No," "I don't know," or remains silent, the parent may assume the child is either stubborn or shy. It is helpful for the parent to remember that for an Introverted child, communication is an energy-intensive activity. For example, if the child has just come home from school, the child may be drained of energy from interacting with others and need time to relax alone before talking about the day.

In addition, the Introverted child needs time to form thoughts before sharing them. It is more helpful for the parent to suggest a topic of conversation before the child enters a social situation than to ask the child questions in the midst of the situation. The parent can also help the child by remembering that an Introverted child is more comfortable talking with one or two people whom the child knows. Pushing the child into groups is more likely to reinforce reticence than to encourage development of communication skills.

Communication That Works

A software company developed a system for holding meetings that incorporated Introverts' preferences for written communication and reflection time and Extraverts' preferences to interact and think out loud. Here is an example.

At 1:30 p.m. a customer contacted the company about a software problem. The team leader immediately e-mailed team members, stating the prob-

the art of dialogue

lem and calling a team meeting for 1:45. The meeting allowed team members to brainstorm and evaluate possible solutions. At 2:00 the team leader ended the meeting with the statement that he would accept additional e-mail input until 2:15. The team leader reviewed the input from both the meeting and follow-up e-mails, sought clarification on an unclear point, and contacted the customer with a recommended solution by 2:30.

APPLYING TYPE: *Notice of agendas for meetings.* The 1:30 e-mail from the leader to team members provided the Introverts a statement of the topic, allowed them to turn their attention away from whatever work they were doing and toward the current problem, and gave them time to reflect so that they were ready to participate in the 1:45 discussion. The meeting gave the Extraverts a time to talk through the problem and respond to the ideas of other team members. After the meeting, some Extraverts continued informal discussions, while Introverts had an opportunity to reflect in private on what they had heard. For Introverts, this reflection often triggers additional ideas. A dean of one university describes herself as an "after-thinker," noting that her best thoughts come after a meeting ends. The after-thoughts of both groups, in this company's approach, could be included in the leader's final considerations.

In general, Introverts are more likely to participate in discussions during meetings when agendas are sent out ahead of time. When they know the topic and have adequate preparation time, Introverts are more comfortable speaking up.

chapter 3 judging and perceiving

Judging and Perceiving are part of *how* a person prefers to receive and give a message in communication. A person's preference on this dichotomy shows up as the last letter (J or P) of a psychological type code.

Attitude/orientation	Extraversion–Introversion	How
Perception function	Sensing–Intuition	What
Judgment function	Thinking–Feeling	What
Attitude/orientation	**Judging–Perceiving**	**How**

One aspect of the Judging and Perceiving preferences relates to a person's preferred lifestyle. People who have a preference for Judging tend to live a planned, structured, and settled lifestyle. People who have a preference for Perceiving tend to live a lifestyle that is spontaneous, flexible, and open to new experiences.

A second aspect of the Judging–Perceiving dichotomy is that it also reflects the part of the personality core that others see first in a person. The language of psychological type theory refers to this second aspect as the outer orientation or the orientation to the external world. In those who prefer Judging, others first see the person's preferred judgment function, whether that is Thinking or Feeling. Others first see a desire for decision making. They hear that the person tends to speak in statements that sound decisive. In those who prefer Perceiving, others first see the person's preferred perception function, whether that is Sensing or Intuition. Others first observe a desire for information gathering. They hear that the person often asks questions and uses statements that sound open ended.

One way to visualize the concept of the outer orientation is to draw arrows as shown in figure 3.1.

figure 3.1
Outer Orientation

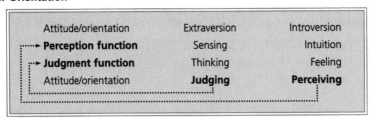

Attitude/orientation	Extraversion	Introversion
Perception function	Sensing	Intuition
Judgment function	Thinking	Feeling
Attitude/orientation	**Judging**	**Perceiving**

The arrow from the Judging preference in the last line points to the third line, which is labeled *judgment function*. The arrow from the Perceiving preference points to the second line, which is labeled *perception function*. For each type—Judging or Perceiving—the arrow points to the part of the personality core that the person most readily reveals to others.

All of us can and do use both of these orientations, but each of us has a natural preference for one over the other. Table 3.1 provides additional information about characteristics of Judging and Perceiving preferences.

Judging and Perceiving in Action

The following stories offer examples of the Judging and Perceiving preferences as they are revealed in communication situations. Listen to the dialogue and watch for related actions to discover clues to the lifestyle preference of each speaker.

Diane and Dave: Spontaneity or Structure

Diane and Dave describe the same work situation from different perspectives and react differently based on their preferences for Judging or Perceiving.

> Diane: When I'd been here at the petroleum company a while, I saw Dave in the cafeteria and said, "Hey, when can we talk?" He responded, "What about?" and I said, "Well, you know, we're going to be working

the art of dialogue

table 3.1
Characteristics of Judging and Perceiving

People Who Prefer Judging	People Who Prefer Perceiving
Tend to want others to know that they	**Tend to want others to know that they**
• are likely to focus on the goal or result	• are likely to focus on the process
• are usually more comfortable once a decision is made even if the decision needs to be changed later	• are usually uncomfortable with premature decisions
• are comfortable with tried and true routines	• maintain interest by doing things in varying ways
• plan a project in steps that have interim or mini closures	• move through a project in a circular or back-and-forth way
In communication, tend to	**In communication, tend to**
• want clear schedules and structures, and definite answers	• want to know the deadline or goal but be allowed to reach it in their own way
• present thorough plans and also have back-up plans	• have difficulty presenting plans to others, since they tend to go where emerging ideas lead them
• experience discomfort with new information received after they think a decision has been made	• welcome new ideas or data until just before the deadline
In interpersonal relationships, may	**In interpersonal relationships, may**
• want clear lines of authority or responsibility	• want freedom to go off task in exploration of interesting and some-times related sidelights
• be impatient with delays or long discussions	• feel put off if discussion is cut off too soon
• assume there are right ways to do things	• assume there are many ways to do things
Often prefer to learn through	**Often prefer to learn through**
• an orderly way at a steady pace	• an experiential or exploratory way, discovering new insights or information

continued next page

table 3.1 *continued*
Characteristics of Judging and Perceiving

People Who Prefer Judging	People Who Prefer Perceiving
Others often observe that they may	**Others often observe that they may**
• speak primarily in statements	• ask questions including rhetorical questions
• use words that end with -ed	• use words that end with -ing
• try to live up to shoulds and oughts	• take a live and let live attitude
• begin work on an assignment or move toward a decision immediately and with great energy but lose interest and energy near the deadline	• take an initial wait-and-see approach to an assignment or decision, but work with a burst of interest and energy as the deadline approaches
Others may be put off because they	**Others may be put off because they**
• often appear to be closed to new information	• bring up new information at the last minute
• decide quickly or appear to decide prematurely	• often appear to be indecisive

together, and I'm going to need information from you to do my job."
He said, "So you want a press release from me." I said I didn't need anything right now, but when it was convenient, I'd like to talk about any
ideas he had. He said that when I had a deadline, I should let him know,
and he would send me something. He also said that after I wrote something about him or his department, I should schedule a meeting with
him in the conference room so he could go over what I wrote before I
sent it out.

Dave: Diane is the kind of person who flits around during work hours
and works during lunch. She asked for a meeting. She hadn't planned a
schedule and couldn't set a time. The bottom line was she wanted to get
a press release out of me. If that's what she wants, she should say so. If
she has a deadline, I will send her the information she needs, if she
knows what that is. I expect her to show me anything she writes about
the chemical engineering department so I can check the accuracy before
it goes out. That's the responsible thing to do.

 LISTENING FOR TYPE CLUES. Diane and Dave describe the
same situation from different perspectives. Diane works in a flexible,
spontaneous, roundabout way. She is comfortable adapting to what

is convenient or suddenly timely. She is also comfortable with a loose structure that does not have set boundaries between work and nonwork activities. These are characteristics of a Perceiving preference.

Dave works in a straightforward way and is concerned with the bottom line. He is most comfortable with planned schedules. He sets clear boundaries between work and play. He takes responsibility and expects the same from others in work and communication. These are characteristics of a Judging preference.

Jane and Paula: Straight Versus Roundabout Paths

Nancy Barger (1991) tells a story about two people who, while watching television in the family room, decide to get a snack.

> Jane: I want some ice cream.
> (Jane goes to the kitchen, takes the ice-cream container from the freezer, sets it on the counter, scoops ice cream into a bowl, puts the container back in the freezer, returns to the family room, and eats the ice cream.)
>
> Paula: That looks good. I think I'll get some.
> (Paula goes to the kitchen, takes the ice-cream container from the freezer, sets it on the counter, and notices that the ice cream is very hard to scoop. At the same time, she notices that the dog's water dish is empty and takes it to the sink to fill it. In the process of setting the dish on the floor, Paula spills the water and grabs a towel to wipe up the spill. She takes the wet towel to the laundry room, sees a pile of other dirty towels, puts them in the washing machine along with detergent and starts the machine. Paula sees that there are clean sheets in the dryer. She folds them and takes them to the linen closet. On the way through the kitchen, she notices that the ice cream is starting to melt and run across the counter. Paula scoops ice cream into a bowl and begins eating it while she wipes up the mess, puts the ice cream container in the freezer, and adds the dishcloth to the load in the washing machine. Paula returns to the family room.)
>
> Jane: Where have you been? I thought you were getting ice cream.
>
> Paula: I did.

LISTENING FOR TYPE CLUES. Both Jane and Paula communicate about one event—getting a bowl of ice cream. For Jane the task is as straightforward as the announcement that she wants the ice cream. Jane expresses characteristics associated with a Judging preference. On the other hand, Paula approaches the task in a circuitous way. She expresses characteristics associated with a Perceiving preference.

APPLYING TYPE: *Similar behavior, different motivation.* When listening for type clues, it is important to note that described behaviors for opposite preferences may sound similar. Careful listening, however, may reveal different motivations for the behavior.

When a woman with a Judging preference heard the story of Jane and Paula, she commented, "I frequently behave like the Perceiving type in this story, but it is because I am working multiple agendas, and when I see an opportunity to complete something on my many lists (mental or written), I do so. On my way to bed I regularly do two loads of laundry, change the towels in the bathroom, feed the cats, and put away the pile of clothes at the foot of my bed."

Like Paula, this woman moves from one task to another, but her motivation for doing so is to complete a number of tasks on her many lists. She wants to come to closure. Paula, on the other hand, had no such motivation. The only task in Paula's mind was to get a dish of ice cream. She had no list or plan to do anything else but took on each task as she became aware of it.

Jill and Rachel: Let's Get Together for Lunch
Psychological type affects the way Jill (ESFP) and Rachel (ISFJ) communicate about lunch plans.

> Jill: Hey, Rachel. Want to meet for lunch today? I have pictures of our kitchen-remodeling project.
>
> Rachel: Let me check my schedule. (Pulls out date book.) I ought to be able to get away if we eat at 11:45, and we go some place nearby.
>
> Jill: Bibi's is only three blocks from here. Oh, and the Cantina is two.
>
> Rachel: Then it's the Cantina.
>
> Jill: When I went there last Tuesday, they'd changed their special. I always liked the Tuesday special.

the art of dialogue

(At 11:30 A.M., Rachel comes to the door of Jill's office.)

Rachel: Are you ready to go?

Jill: As soon as I finish entering these last two class registrations into the database.

Rachel: You can do that after lunch, can't you?

Jill: The deadline is noon.

Rachel: If we don't leave now, we won't get into Bibi's. It takes ten minutes to get there, and they fill up by 11:45.

Jill: Didn't you say we were going to the Cantina?

Rachel: You didn't want to go there.

Jill: Bibi's is fine, if that's where you'd rather go. If you're in a hurry, go ahead, and I'll meet you.

Rachel: You sure push the deadlines.

Jill: Oh, you know how it is. The student has to get permission from the instructor to register, and the instructor doesn't get back to the student, but somehow all the pieces come together when they have to.

LISTENING FOR TYPE CLUES. Jill, who has a preference for Perceiving, is comfortable making a spur-of-the moment lunch date. She quickly offers alternatives that meet Rachel's requirement for a place nearby. When Rachel changes the location, Jill is flexible. When Rachel is uncomfortable with Jill's last-minute work, Jill adapts the plan, telling Rachel to go ahead of her. In her work Jill trusts that she will have the information she needs before or by the last minute and that she will meet the deadline.

Rachel, who has a preference for Judging, checks her schedule before she makes a commitment. She sets parameters and includes the time needed to get from the office to the restaurant in the plan for lunch. She makes a decision about a restaurant based on the location information Jill gives her. Then, when Jill makes a comment about the restaurant, Rachel concludes that Jill does not want to go there. She quickly acts on her conclusion and decides on a new plan—to go to a different restaurant.

APPLYING TYPE: *Procrastination.* A common misconception is that people who have a Perceiving preference are procrastinators and miss deadlines. Procrastination is type related, but it is not a particular characteristic of Perceiving types. All people procrastinate on those things that require the use of a less-preferred attitude or function.

All types usually meet deadlines, but different types may follow different paths to get there. People who have a Judging preference tend to be energetic about a project when it is first assigned. They start work right away, and methodically make their way toward the deadline. Judging types often report that energy wanes as they approach the deadline. They say that they just want to get it done.

People who have a Perceiving preference may wait for a bit before beginning a newly assigned project. They may delay starting because they are attending to tasks that have more immediate deadlines, and so have a higher priority. The waiting period also allows them time to gather information. Perceiving types often report that they "mull over the ideas" or "wait to see what comes up." As the deadline approaches and pieces come together and possibilities become apparent, Perceiving types may experience a surge of energy.

In this story, Jill was aware of the deadline. She did not leave for lunch until she met it, but the last-minute rush to meet the deadline did not upset her. If Rachel had faced the same circumstances, she likely would have felt stressed.

Shaundra and Kelli: The Process of Writing

Shaundra and Kelli are classmates who approach a writing assignment in different ways.

Teacher: On Thursday I want you to turn in the topic of your next paper. You have until next Tuesday to gather information on note cards and write a thesis statement. Your outline is due Wednesday, and the first draft is due Friday. You will have time to revise your paper before the final copy is due the following Friday.

Kelli: (after class) Hey, Shaundra, a bunch of us are going to hang out this weekend. Want to come?

Shaundra: Yeah, right. I'd love to, if it weren't for that assignment we just got.

Kelli: It isn't due for two weeks.

Shaundra: But we have to turn in the thesis statement Tuesday and an outline Wednesday. I hate deadlines like that.

Kelli: It's just a summary statement and outline. It isn't like you have to write the whole paper.

Shaundra: How else do you know the thesis, or what's in the outline? I've got a topic, but I sure don't know where it's going, and that's what teachers want in a thesis statement. I wish they'd just give a list of stuff to hand in at the end, like draft and thesis statement and note cards and outline. Then I could write a first draft, figure out what's missing and find the notes, then arrange stuff to make an outline, and find a conclusion. But, no! They have all these deadlines, and they put them in backwards order.

Kelli: Why do you make it so hard? The assignment works for me. If I do the thesis statement and outline tonight and make some notes tomorrow and the next day, I can check off all three things so the weekend is free.

LISTENING FOR TYPE CLUES. Kelli is comfortable with the teacher's assignment schedule. She knows where to begin right away, and she can check off each step as she completes it. She is comfortable beginning with a thesis statement and making an outline before she writes a first draft. Kelli's reaction is characteristic of a person with a Judging preference.

In contrast, Shaundra is uncomfortable with a structured schedule. She needs to let thoughts flow in random order before she structures them into an outline or formulates a main idea. Shaundra's reaction is characteristic of a person with a Perceiving preference.

APPLYING TYPE: *Starting to write.* John DiTiberio and George Jensen (1995), in *Writing and Personality: Finding Your Voice, Your Style, Your Way,* describe characteristics of each preference as it relates to the process of writing. They say that people who prefer Judging tend to

- limit topics quickly,
- schedule steps which allow for small closures throughout the writing process,
- write deductively, often stating a conclusion in the first paragraph,

- use revisions to broaden information that is presented,
- present material in a direct, forceful way, then soften it in revisions.

DiTiberio and Jensen state that people who prefer Perceiving tend to
- select broad topics,
- write spontaneously in bursts of energy,
- write inductively, perhaps alluding to a conclusion or ending with further questions,
- use revisions to narrow the focus of information, and
- overqualify statements, then edit out excess words in revisions.

Children and Type

As with Extraversion and Introversion, we often observe characteristics associated with Judging and Perceiving even in young children. Those who have a Judging preference tend to be concerned with external order, rules, and tasks. Those who have a Perceiving preference tend to be concerned with internal order, varying routine, and process.

People with Judging and Perceiving preferences also manage time differently. Those who have a Judging preference tend to schedule time. They may begin a project energetically but wear down as they continue through it. Those who have a Perceiving preference tend to adapt to time. They may have less energy for the beginning of a project, but after a period of mulling it over, they energetically bring the project together as they approach the deadline. In the following story we see the effects of different time management preferences as two sisters discuss homework with their mother.

Madalyn and Kaitlyn: Time Management

Madalyn (twelve years old) and Kaitlyn (ten years old) are sisters. Each has a different way of dealing with a homework assignment.

Mom: Are you sure you're done with your homework, Madalyn?

Madalyn: I've done tomorrow's work.

Mom: You said your history teacher assigned a research paper.

Madalyn: I'm thinking about it. I've got several ideas.

36

Mom: You can start making some notes even if you don't know how the whole paper will come out in the end.

Madalyn: What if I started one thing and then changed my mind? I'd just waste my time.

Mom: How long do you think you're going to put this off?

Madalyn: It's not due 'til next Friday. I've got every night next week to do it.

Mom: Every night? Your choir concert is Thursday.

Madalyn: So I'll do it Tuesday and Wednesday. Once I've figured it out, it won't take long to write it.

Mom: Remember, your cousin's birthday is Tuesday, and you also have an essay for English class due on Wednesday.

Madalyn: So I'll do the English essay over the weekend and the history paper Monday and Wednesday. No big deal. Now, I'm going to Paige's house. OK?

Kaitlyn: How come she gets to go to her friend's house, and I have to stay here and do my homework?

Mom: Kaitlyn, you've been working ever since you got home from school. Maybe you should take a break.

Kaitlyn: I have to do this science project. Do we have any note cards? I need to make labels.

Mom: I don't know. When's your project due?

Kaitlyn: Next Tuesday.

Mom: Well then, you have time. We can get note cards tomorrow.

Kaitlyn: But I know now what I want to say. If I don't write it now, I might forget, and then I'd have to think it up all over again. Anyway, we might have a big math assignment tomorrow.

 LISTENING FOR TYPE CLUES. We would not want to leap to a conclusion about the psychological types of children such as Madalyn and Kaitlyn. Still, we get hints that if we were to observe them over a period of time, and if later in their lives they were to identify their own type preferences, we might see patterns of characteristics associated with a Perceiving preference for Madalyn and a Judging preference for Kaitlyn.

Madalyn meets the immediate deadline for homework that is due the next day, but she does not feel pressure about a future deadline. She indicates that she is thinking about her research topic and considering options—for her, part of the information-gathering process. Madalyn feels that starting work too soon may result in wasted effort because she may have to rework parts of the project. She sees waiting to start until after she gathers and sorts through information as the most efficient way to work. She responds favorably to her mother's attempts to help her plan from the deadline to the absolutely necessary starting point. For Madalyn, changing the schedule is no big deal. As she receives additional information, she is flexible in adapting her plan to include an earlier starting point that accommodates additional activities. Madalyn expresses characteristics associated with a Perceiving preference.

Kaitlyn feels pressure about a deadline as soon as she receives an assignment. She immediately seeks ways to complete as many pieces of the project as possible. Her mother's suggestions that she take a break or wait until tomorrow to make labels are sources of stress rather than comfort. Kaitlyn expresses characteristics that are associated with a Judging preference.

APPLYING TYPE: *Parenting a child with a Judging or Perceiving preference.* Telling a child who has a Perceiving preference that the child must start a project immediately after it is assigned in order to make the deadline may be seen by the youngster as a lie. The child knows that he or she can wait to start the project and still complete it on time. Elizabeth Murphy (1992), in *The Developing Child*, suggests that it is more productive to help the child determine a starting time by working backward from the deadline. The parent can also remind the child of upcoming events that might affect the schedule.

Murphy also suggests that a child who has a Judging preference needs to complete work in order to relax. If a parent sees a child working late and tells the child to go to bed and finish the work in the morning, the child is likely to lie awake worrying. Asking what help the child needs, offering the child a cup of hot chocolate, and creating a comfortable work environment are ways that parents can effectively support a child with a Judging preference.

the art of dialogue

Communication That Works

Marcus has a preference for Judging. His wife, Cecelia, has a preference for Perceiving. For several years family vacations were a source of conflict.

Marcus took pride in his organizational and planning skills as he prepared travel plans. He organized a daily schedule that took into account interests he knew family members had, days and hours of each activity, and proximity of locations. He planned a budget that provided greatest value for the amount of money the family could afford to spend. He made lodging reservations so that the family was assured of a place to stay even if they arrived during a peak travel time. Vacations that Marcus planned seldom had unwelcome surprises.

In spite of his best planning and his attention to including activities based on family interests, Cecelia and the children complained that vacations were for Marcus, not for them. The conflict came to a head one day as the family drove toward a destination listed on Marcus's schedule. Cecelia and the children spotted a sign to a tourist site.

Cecelia: Oh look, Marcus! Let's stop there. It's just a little way from this next exit.

Marcus: It's not on the schedule.

Cecelia: Why not? This site is the kind of place the children and I enjoy.

Marcus: It wasn't listed in the information I had, so I didn't know about it.

Cecelia: But now we do know about it, and we're right here.

Marcus: If we stop, we won't get to our destination for tonight, where we already have a reservation, and we won't be able to do all the things we have planned for tomorrow.

(When the family returned from their trip and friends asked about it, Cecelia and the children talked about the missed adventure. Cecelia and Marcus decided they needed to discuss the conflict, and Cecelia described her frustration.)

Cecelia: The problem is the rigidity of the schedule. There's no way to do anything on the spur of the moment. Sometimes things just come along that we want to do, but we're stuck following the schedule.

(Marcus offered to try a change in his travel planning.)

Marcus: What if the vacation schedule had a few blocks of unscheduled time? Would that do what you want?

Cecelia: It's worth a try. I do appreciate much of your planning, like knowing which days a site is open so we don't arrive when it's closed, and knowing where sites are located so we don't spend most of our time traveling between places rather than enjoying the activities themselves. But sometimes we're scheduled for several activities on a day when we'd rather have a leisurely day. Or sometimes we just don't feel like doing the activity that's scheduled for a particular day. I'd like more flexibility.

Marcus thought about Cecelia's request and tried an additional change in his way of planning. Instead of organizing a daily schedule, he created a database of available options. The database still included planning information Marcus wanted—days and hours, locations, costs. Now, however, the family could choose each day from the list of things to do and develop a schedule for that day. As they discovered other available activities, they could add these to the list as possible choices. As a result of the discussion between Cecelia and Marcus and the changes in planning procedures that Marcus made, tensions in the family eased, and vacations were more enjoyable for all family members.

LISTENING FOR TYPE CLUES. Marcus, who has a preference for Judging, wants planning and organization in his life. When he takes a vacation, he uses his organizational skills to gather information and decide on schedules that help him avoid unwelcome surprises. The structure of his plans provides a comfort zone for the travel days when his everyday methods, routines, and structures are altered. Establishing that comfort zone allows Marcus to relax and enjoy the vacation.

Cecelia, who has a preference for Perceiving, wants flexibility and spontaneity. Work and family demands often require organization, planning, and adherence to schedules for those who prefer Perceiving as well as for those who prefer Judging. When Cecelia takes a vacation, she finds freedom and refreshment in leaving behind usual schedules, adapting to new information, and making spur-of-the-moment decisions.

Through their discussion, Marcus and Cecelia recognize the differences in their Judging and Perceiving preferences. Cecelia gives appreciation to Marcus for his organizational skills. Marcus offers compromises that meet the needs of both, such as scheduling unscheduled time and creating a database to guide planning rather than preparing a fixed plan. Their understanding of type differences result in effective communication between Marcus and Cecelia and more enjoyable family vacations.

chapter 4 sensing and intuition

Two fundamental mental processes form the core of psychological type. They identify *what* kind of content a person prefers to emphasize first in a message. One fundamental process is perception, which involves gathering information through the functions of Sensing or Intuition. The function shows up as the second letter (S or N) in a psychological type code.

Attitude/orientation	Extraversion–Introversion	How
Perception function	**Sensing–Intuition**	**What**
Judgment function	Thinking–Feeling	What
Attitude/orientation	Judging–Perceiving	How

People who prefer Sensing tend to take in information through the five senses. They are likely to be most interested in and trust what is real, concrete, and practical, for example, facts, details, and experience. People who prefer Intuition go beyond what they take in through the senses and tend to take in information through the use of insight, inspiration, and imagination. They are likely to be most interested in and trust possibilities, symbols, concepts, and underlying meanings.

All of us can and do use both Sensing and Intuition to gather information, but each of us has a natural preference for one over the other. Table 4.1 (44–45) provides additional information about characteristics of Sensing and Intuition.

table 4.1
Characteristics of Sensing and Intuition

People Who Prefer Sensing	People Who Prefer Intuition
Tend to want others to know that they	**Tend to want others to know that they**
• are likely to look for practical applications • orient to the present and past • trust experience • respect what is proven	• are likely to look for immediate and long-range implications • orient toward the future • trust hunches and inspirations • use imagination to create something
In communication, tend to	**In communication, tend to**
• first want and give information that is real, concrete, practical, factual, and specific • want step-by-step information or directions • remember facts and details of events • see what is • pay attention to the richness of a fact for its own sake	• first want and give information that is insightful, opens possibilities, uses the imagination, presents an overview or synthesis, and shows patterns • want guidelines with freedom to find their own way to get information • remember impressions or the essence of events • read between the lines • pay more attention to the relationship between facts or implications of facts than to the facts themselves
In interpersonal relationships, may	**In interpersonal relationships, may**
• be impatient with vague, inaccurate, or unrealistic possibilities • tune out in discussions of theoretical ideas • see the source of conflict in specific details of particular events	• be impatient with discussions that seem too literal or narrowly focused • switch off if overloaded with details • see the source of conflict in differing interpretations of events or in patterns of events
Often prefer to learn through	**Often prefer to learn by through**
• building a body of evidence from the details to the theory • memorizing • acquiring knowledge for pragmatic reasons • starting at the beginning of a learning task and moving straight through	• starting with the theory and then relating the details to the idea • understanding concepts and finding reasons • acquiring knowledge for its own sake • starting the learning task anywhere and leaping around or going back to the beginning when it is needed

table 4.1 *continued*
Characteristics of Sensing and Intuition

People Who Prefer Sensing	People Who Prefer Intuition
Others often observe that they may	Others often observe that they may
• ask what and how questions	• ask what if and why questions
• speak of what is or what has been	• speak of what might be, what the main issue is, and what jumped out
• give precise descriptions	• use "sort of" and general impression descriptions
• give factual statements	• give analogies and metaphors
• be cautious not to go beyond the actual	• exaggerate
• get stuck on a single fact or detail and not always hear the rest of the statement	• anticipate words and not always hear others out
Others may be put off because they	Others may be put off because they
• may appear to be literal, narrow-minded, or stuck in a rut	• may appear to be ungrounded, going off on a tangent, or impractical

Sensing and Intuition in Action

The stories that follow illustrate Sensing and Intuition in action. Listen particularly for the kind of content each speaker presents. Those who prefer Sensing are likely to present specific facts and details, while those who prefer Intuition are more likely to speak about general concepts and possibilities.

Diane and Dave: What Is Information?

Because Diane and Dave differ in their preferences between Sensing and Intuition, they have different ideas about what constitutes information.

> Diane: Dave's chemical engineering department at our petroleum company is working on new products and product improvement. It's exactly the kind of thing that can create positive publicity for the company. People are interested in reading about what's new and improved. Dave thinks he can't give me any information because he doesn't have all the pieces in place, and the project isn't finished, but people don't need all the details. Good marketing and publicity builds anticipation and excitement for what's possible. We can give a general idea of the direction for the future so people are looking forward to what we will be able to offer.

Dave: Diane wants to release half-baked ideas as stories that represent the petroleum company. If you don't have all the facts, people speculate about all kinds of crazy things. They expect products the company can't deliver. Publicity needs to be accurate and realistic. Otherwise, it can result in a negative impact on the company.

LISTENING FOR TYPE CLUES. Diane is most interested in possibilities, an overview of general ideas, and imagining the future. For her a general idea is information. She exhibits characteristics associated with a preference for Intuition. For Dave, a general idea is only speculation, not information. He is most interested in accurate, specific, factual information about what is known at the present time. He exhibits characteristics associated with a preference for Sensing.

Mara and Her Supervisor: How Does This Computer Work?

Mara (ISFJ) is a typist in a company that prints technical manuals. She transferred to a new facility in the company and told a friend about her initial interaction with her new supervisor.

Mara: My supervisor showed me the new computers and software. He kept going from one thing to another—things I'll almost never need—but, he was so excited and kept saying, "Oh, let me show you something else. The possibilities are endless." He talked on and on for thirty minutes before he even came up for air or noticed I was there. Finally, after half an hour he asked, "Do you have any questions?" I just looked at him and said, "I've looked all over this machine while you've talked, and I don't see the switch. How do you turn it on? What are the passwords? What are the steps to enter a secure document?"

LISTENING FOR TYPE CLUES. Mara's supervisor is excited by the new computers and the many possibilities the software offers. He jumps from one interesting feature to another, in no particular order as far as Mara can discern. We can hypothesize that he may have a preference for Intuition. One possibility suggests another, which suggests still another.

Mara, who has a Sensing preference, wants to start at the beginning and proceed step by step through the computers' features that have practical applications for her.

46

APPLYING TYPE: *What is information?* Sensing and Intuition preferences influence what kind of information a person tends to send or wants to receive in a message. If a person receives information for which the individual is listening, that person is likely to say that good communication has occurred. If the individual does not receive the desired information, the person is likely to express frustration and may conclude that the sender of the message does not know how to communicate.

Mara's supervisor likely believes he is giving her information. After all, he is telling her what he would like to hear. Because of her preference for Sensing, she becomes impatient and frustrated when she does not get the data that she needs to do her work. From Mara's perspective, the supervisor does not know how to communicate information.

Erik, Tyrone, and Dierdre: What Time Is It?

> Erik (ENTP), Tyrone (ESTP), and Dierdre (ISTJ) purchase tickets for a 7:15 p.m. movie. As they walk through the lobby toward the theater, Erik stops.
>
> **Erik:** Hey, wait a minute, you guys. I want something from the concession stand.
>
> **Dierdre:** I'd like a large buttered popcorn.
>
> **Tyrone:** Look at that line. I don't know that we'd get through it before the movie starts. What time is it?
>
> **Erik:** A little after 7:00.
>
> **Dierdre:** It's 7:07.

LISTENING FOR TYPE CLUES. Erik, who has a preference for Intuition, begins with the concepts rather than the specifics of food from the concession stand and of time. He wants something from the concession stand, and he gives the approximate time.

Tyrone and Dierdre both have a preference for Sensing. Tyrone notices the long line at the concession stand and comments on it. He seems to sense that Erik has not noticed this fact. Dierdre is specific about time and the food she wants—the kind (popcorn), the flavor (buttered), and the size (large).

APPLYING TYPE: *Clues that point to preferences.* Clues to type preferences can appear in any conversation, but the best clues tend to show up in informal conversation about relatively trivial matters. We express type preferences most naturally in situations when nothing hangs on doing the *right* thing or making the *right* choice. Because any person can and does use both options on a dichotomy, it is generally not as helpful to listen for type clues in situations in which a person is required to use the skills associated with a particular preference. These situations do not offer choice. Informal conversation about relatively trivial matters usually does include real choice.

Wyatt, Elaine, and Dan: Possibilities or Applications

Wyatt (ESFJ), Elaine (ENFP), and Dan (ISTP) teach in the same school and car pool to continuing education classes at a nearby university. Wyatt takes one class, while Elaine and Dan are in another class. The three react differently to their professors' teaching approaches.

> **Wyatt:** This class is a waste of time. I took it to get specific examples of things I can use in my classroom, but this professor spends the whole time on "what if" and "maybe" and "it might be interesting to think about." I wonder if he's ever been in a real classroom.

> **Elaine:** You'd get a lot of specific examples in our class. That's all it is— one specific example after another. Last week I stopped the instructor and said I needed to know what idea she was trying to illustrate with the examples. She said she was coming to that. I guess sometimes she does state a theme at the end of the class, but I don't know what to listen for when she doesn't start with an overview.

> **Dan:** I respect this instructor's teaching skills. She says just what you need to know. She doesn't throw in extraneous stuff, and her tests are fair—no surprises.

LISTENING FOR TYPE CLUES. We can hypothesize that the professor of Wyatt's class has a preference for Intuition. The professor talks about theory and possibilities. But Wyatt has a preference for Sensing and wants specific and concrete information instead of broad concepts and what-ifs.

the art of dialogue

The instructor of Elaine's and Dan's class may have a preference for Sensing. The instructor appears to build from specific examples to a conclusion, which is a typical practice for those who prefer Sensing. Elaine, who has a preference for Intuition, needs to hear the main idea first. Then she can relate the specific examples to the main idea. Dan, who has a preference for Sensing, appreciates the instructor's focus on specifics.

APPLYING TYPE: *Speaking to both Sensing and Intuitive types.* Any group is likely to include both people who prefer Intuition and those who prefer Sensing. People who prefer Intuition usually want to know the big picture first, then relate the details or specific examples to the main idea. Those who prefer Sensing often want to build from the specifics to a conclusion. So, how can a speaker address the needs of listeners with these opposite preferences? A familiar rule is helpful.

1) Say what you're going to say.

2) Say it.

3) Say what you've said.

In Step 1, speakers give an overview or main idea for those who prefer Intuition. In Step, 2 they provide specific details. In Step 3, speakers summarize details into a conclusion for those who prefer Sensing.

Zach and Johnna: Is It Art?

Zach (ISTJ) and Johnna (INTJ) both enjoy visiting art galleries, but they are attracted to different pieces of art and notice different aspects in the artworks.

Johnna: The look of the man in this portrait is haunting.

Zach: I like the portrait of the eighteenth-century noblewoman better. The wrinkles in the face are right for a seventy-five-year-old woman in the 1750s. Look at the precise stitching on the collar that frames her face.

Johnna: She looks stiff—more like a corpse than a live person. In the portrait of the man, I see the eyes.

Zach: In a good portrait the eyes should look at you no matter from what angle you view the picture. That man doesn't look at anything, and his head is tilted at an unnatural angle compared to the torso. A body doesn't twist that way.

Johnna: I think the eyes see something in the distance. The body is straining to see something clearly. The man looks like the kind of person who has ideas that others consider twisted. He must be a philosopher.

LISTENING FOR TYPE CLUES. Zach, who has a preference for Sensing, is attracted first to details, particularly those that reflect reality. Johnna, who has a preference for Intuition, is first attracted to aspects of the artwork that engage her imagination. She thinks of possibilities that go beyond the actual depiction.

APPLYING TYPE: *Sensing and Intuition in creativity and fine arts.* A common misconception about type theory is that primarily Intuitive types appreciate fine arts and are creative. However, all types can appreciate the arts and be creative. As illustrated in the dialogue between Zach and Johnna, different types generally focus on different aspects of art. (For more discussion about type and creativity, see part 5 of this book.)

Children and Type

Unlike the attitudes and orientations of Extraversion–Introversion or Judging–Perceiving, the functions such as Sensing and Intuition may not be readily apparent in young children. All children see the world in fairly concrete terms when they are very young. In general, children do not develop cognitive skills to understand abstract concepts for several years. Even so, we often see some clues to possible type preferences. In the following dialogue, a three-year-old shows concern for accuracy of a detail.

Three-year-old Monty and his mother are visiting a neighbor. Through Monty's response to a statement his mother makes, we can get a hint of a possible preference between Sensing and Intuition.

Mother: (to Monty) Can you tell her what we're going to do tomorrow?

Monty: What?

Mother: Are we going to the apple festival?

Monty: (frowning and stamping his foot) We're going to the Applejack Festival.

the art of dialogue

LISTENING FOR TYPE CLUES. We would not want to leap to a conclusion about Monty's type based on one brief incident. Also, he is too young for us to draw conclusions about his type. Still, we get a hint that if we were to observe him over a period of time, and if later in his life he were to identify his type preference, we might see patterns of characteristics associated with a Sensing preference. In this incident, Monty corrects his mother when she uses a generic term rather than the exact name of the festival. Monty is aware of and focused on detail, even though he is just a toddler.

APPLYING TYPE: *Reality and imagination in young children.* Parents may see and hear clues to Sensing and Intuition preferences as they observe young children at play. Children who have a Sensing preference tend to stay close to reality when they play with toys, while children who have an Intuitive preference are more likely to play with toys in an imaginative way. If a Sensing child plays with a set of toy dishes, the child may use a cup to drink a real or imagined beverage, or to pour, measure, or scoop. An Intuitive child may use a cup in all these ways, too, but may also use the cup as a boat or as a bed for a small doll or insect. The child may turn the cup upside down and use it as a springboard for a toy acrobat or as a secret cave for an animal. The cup may become a container for an imaginary magic potion that can conjure up dragons or transport someone to a fantasyland.

Sensing children often enjoy books of facts, such as the Richard Scary series for young children, or biographies and real-life adventure stories for older children. Intuitive children more often seek books with imaginative stories.

Children with Sensing preferences expect accuracy in their books. One three-year-old pointed out an error every time his parent read his book about the gingerbread man. On one page of the book the illustrator had changed the order of the colors for the gingerbread man's gumdrop buttons.

Communication That Works

Ed (INTP) was a biochemist who taught in the agricultural college of a large university. He was knowledgeable in his field and enjoyed teaching, but for several years he received some of the lowest ratings on student evaluations of faculty. One spring a colleague presented a seminar to the ag faculty on psychological type. The colleague had administered the Myers-Briggs Type Indicator® instrument to many of the students and found the students reported predominately Sensing preferences.

Ed, who preferred Intuition, was intrigued by what he heard and spent the summer revising his curriculum and syllabus to address the needs of his Sensing students.

The next semester Ed's students responded extremely well to the changes in his teaching style. When the semester ended, the faculty ethics committee was shocked that Ed, who had been receiving low ratings, suddenly received nearly the highest student ratings among faculty. The committee wrongly accused Ed of bribing his students to give positive ratings.

APPLYING TYPE: *Teaching to Sensing and Intuitive preferences.* Because teaching involves presenting information, it is the province of the Sensing and Intuition functions. Table 4.2 offers suggestions to enhance communication in teaching situations.

table 4.2
Suggestions for Teaching to People Preferring Sensing and Intuition

People Who Prefer Sensing	People Who Prefer Intuition
• Introduce the topic with a statement about its usefulness and practicality	• Introduce the topic with a statement about the concept or big picture
• Present facts and realistic details, paying attention to parts of the whole and steps of the process	• Present options and possibilities
• Provide thorough, concrete data	• Provide analogies, symbols, and theoretical models
• Allow the listener to build a body of evidence step-by-step from the details to the theory and to interact with the information through practical, hands-on experience	• Allow the listener to attach details, facts, and steps onto the conceptual idea and to interact with the information through imagination and insights
• Recognize that the listener may ask and tune into what and how questions	• Recognize that the listener may ask and tune into what if and why questions
• Provide written and oral directions, with time to try activities, ask questions, and receive feedback before expecting completion	• Provide opportunity for listeners to restate directions in their own words and carry out directions creatively
• Know that the listeners are likely to define intelligence as soundness of understanding, comprehending specifics thoroughly	• Know that the listeners are likely to define intelligence as quickness of understanding, grasping global concepts immediately

the art of dialogue

The effective communication of information in teaching situations includes three elements: the goal, the content, and the method. Psychological type does not set the goal nor determine the content. However, type does help identify aspects of the method that can make the communication effective and heard.

People often find themselves in teaching situations, whether as a teacher in a classroom, as a parent, as a professional with clients, as a businessperson with customers, or as an employee with co-workers. Being aware of the influence of Sensing and Intuition preferences in teaching situations can help the teacher communicate the desired content to reach the intended goal.

chapter 5 thinking and feeling

The core of psychological type includes two fundamental mental processes that identify *what* kind of content a person prefers to emphasize first in a message. The first fundamental process is perception, and the second is judgment. The two alternatives of the judgment dichotomy are Thinking and Feeling, which relate to decision making. This preference shows up as the third letter (T or F) in a psychological type code.

Attitude/orientation	Extraversion–Introversion	How
Perception function	Sensing–Intuition	What
Judgment function	Thinking–Feeling	What
Attitude/orientation	Judging–Perceiving	How

People who prefer Thinking tend to make decisions based on objective, logical analysis of cause and effect or through the application of principles. People who prefer Feeling tend to make decisions based on subjective person-centered values or the impact of the decision on others.

As with the attitudes and functions covered earlier, all of us can and do use both preferences in making decisions, but each of us has a natural preference for one over the other. Table 5.1 (pages 56–57) provides additional information about characteristics of Thinking and Feeling types.

table 5.1
Characteristics of Thinking and Feeling

People Who Prefer Thinking	People Who Prefer Feeling
Tend to want others to know that they	**Tend to want others to know that they**
• typically focus first on principles or objective standards • use logical analysis of cause and effect, critique, and are concerned with truth and justice	• typically focus first on relationships and harmony between people and values • consider what is most important or best for themselves or people who are important to them
In communication, tend to	**In communication, tend to**
• want logical reasons before accepting new ideas • weigh pros and cons • enjoy the give and take of debate to the extent of being willing to advocate for either side • accept conflict as normal	• agree with ideas of others before examining the ideas • seek consensus or greatest good and look for what they have in common with others or what they all can agree on • find the give and take of arguments upsetting but are able to see both sides of an issue • prefer cooperation
In interpersonal relationships, may	**In interpersonal relationships, may**
• be skeptical of personal attention or too great a show of appreciation or positive feedback • be unaware of the personal needs of others • mentally step outside a situation to look at it objectively even if they are participants in the situation	• work most effectively when they receive positive feedback and personal appreciation • recognize the personal needs of others • mentally walk in another's shoes to look at a situation even if they are not participants in the situation
Often prefer to learn through	**Often prefer to learn through**
• teachers or trainers who follow a logical outline • critique and debate of challenging ideas or practical problems • testing skills or knowledge and in competitive situations	• teachers or trainers who are warm and welcoming • stories that illustrate the concept and are personally relevant • working cooperatively on projects

table 5.1 *continued*
Characteristics of Thinking and Feeling

People Who Prefer Thinking	People Who Prefer Feeling
Others often observe that they may	**Others often observe that they may**
• speak about "what makes sense" or "how to improve"	• speak about "what feels right" or "what I appreciate"
• say "I think"	• say "I feel"
• seek compromise	• seek collaboration
• give little facial expression or body language feedback to a speaker	• give feedback to a speaker through facial expressions such as smiles or frowns or through body language such as nodding in agreement
• ask questions or challenge ideas to test knowledge and competence of a speaker	• discuss a problem or check credentials with a third party rather than speaking directly to a speaker
• be unimpressed by how or what others decided	• ask how or what others decided
• be put off by personal conversations	• build relationships in the course of work and include personal and work matters in conversations
• be brief and to the point, compact and efficient in communications	• ramble and repeat self
• use objective logic ("if this, then that")	• tell personal stories
Others may be put off because they	**Others may be put off because they**
• often appear to be critical when they move first to examining ideas and suggesting improvements	• often appear as lacking backbone when they naturally seek inclusion of everyone's contributions and push for consensus
• are direct to the extent of seeming insensitive to others	• use flattery that may be perceived as manipulation by others
• use dark humor or sharp wit that may be misunderstood by others	• take things personally at the risk of becoming overly emotional

Thinking and Feeling in Action

The following stories and dialogues offer examples of how Thinking and Feeling preferences affect communication.

Diane and Dave: Personal Relationships in the Workplace

Diane and Dave express different views on relationships in the workplace and approaches to work.

Diane: When Dave didn't speak up in the interdepartmental meetings at our petroleum company, I could understand his not wanting to talk to someone he didn't know, so I asked him if we could have lunch together. I felt it would help if he got to know me, and I wanted to know him better. We actually have a lot in common. We both have degrees in chemistry, and we've both worked in chemical engineering departments. I assumed that after he got to know me, he'd be more willing to trust me with information. After all, we both want what's good for this company, and we're more likely to help the image of the company if we cooperate with each other on publicity.

Dave: Diane would be better off if she'd stick to business. She wanted to get acquainted over lunch. As I see it, work is work, and personal life is personal life. People who confuse the two lose objectivity when conflicts inevitably happen. As a matter of fact, I'm skeptical about Diane's ability to critically analyze what she hears. From what I see, if the right person states an idea, then she gets all enthusiastic without even thinking about it. I'd be more willing to give her information if she were straightforward and logical.

LISTENING FOR TYPE CLUES. Diane focuses first on relationships and includes both personal and work matters in conversations. She attempts to understand a situation by putting herself in another's place, looks for what people have in common, and prefers to work cooperatively on projects. These are characteristics of the Feeling preference.

Dave makes a clear distinction between personal and work relationships. He is put off by personal conversations in the workplace. He uses analysis to consider a situation and expects others to critique information and look for what makes sense and conveys truth. These are characteristics of the Thinking preference.

Two Workers: Evaluating a Situation

When we are aware of type clues, we hear them all around us in everyday speech. A type-aware jogger overheard the following bit of dialogue from two workers as she passed a construction zone. The jogger recognized clues to possible differences in Thinking and Feeling preferences through the workers' conversation.

the art of dialogue

Worker 1: Too bad Jim got fired. He was a good worker.

Worker 2: The way he wanted to do that excavation seemed reasonable, but the boss couldn't see the sense of it.

Worker 1: Yeah. There was a lack of understanding on both sides.

Worker 2: The boss has his own way to do things, and he's the boss.

LISTENING FOR TYPE CLUES. We can hypothesize that worker 1 may have a preference for Feeling. He begins with a statement about a person ("He [Jim] was a good worker") and expresses sympathy that he got fired ("too bad"). He evaluates the situation from a middle ground, almost speaking as a mediator who sees that both sides typically contribute to disharmony.

We can also hypothesize that worker 2 may have a preference for Thinking. He begins with a statement about a task and method ("the way he wanted to do that excavation") and evaluates the situation in terms of what seems reasonable and makes sense. Then, he lets go of the situation with an objective statement ("The boss has his own way to do things, and he's the boss").

APPLYING TYPE: *Practicing listening skills.* We are most likely to want to use our knowledge of type to enhance communication in relationships that matter to us, both in work settings and in our personal lives. Sometimes, however, relationships that matter most are also ones in which it is difficult to learn and practice the skills of listening for type clues. Relationships that matter may be overlaid with emotions or social intricacies or demands of the task. While we do not want to go so far as to become eavesdroppers, we may find that we can learn and practice skills in listening for type clues by paying attention to casual conversations that do not carry significance for us.

Steve, Carter, and Nan: Getting Down to Work

Steve (ENTJ) is the leader of a work team. Carter (ENFP) and Nan (ISFJ) are team members. Based on their preferences, they view acknowledging team members' contributions differently than their team leader.

Steve: The purpose of today's meeting is to hammer out parts two and five of the current project. You all know this needs to go out by the end of the week, so I've scheduled an hour to get it wrapped up. As I see it, part two will be improved by . . . (Steve provides suggestions). Am I right? What do you think?

Carter: (whispering to Nan) Every meeting starts the same way. He criticizes whatever we did last time, then says, "Here's what you need to do to fix it." I knocked myself out for him on this one, and he doesn't even care. I'm not doing any more. If he wants it done, he can do it himself.

Nan: (whispering to Carter) I wouldn't mind helping if he'd appreciate what we do. We've worked hard, and it's like we haven't done anything. I don't have anything to contribute to this meeting.

LISTENING FOR TYPE CLUES. Steve, who has a preference for Thinking, values efficiency. He has a natural tendency to get right to the task—to critique and suggest improvements. He is not inclined to review what has already been done. He would consider that a waste of time. He assumes people know he appreciates their work because he has not pointed out any glaring errors.

Before they move into the next phase of work, Carter and Nan—who have preferences for Feeling—have a need to be recognized and appreciated for the work they and others on the team have done. They are concerned about the work, but they first value harmony and respectfulness among team members.

APPLYING TYPE: *Efficiency and appreciation.* A leader who has a Thinking preference may be able to move through a task most efficiently by taking a moment to offer a word of appreciation. That moment can avert resistance—sometimes sustained resistance—which Feeling types may throw in the way of the current task if they feel unappreciated. Steve probably could have brought Carter and Nan on board if he had reworded his opening statement as follows:

We've done good work on the current project. Thanks to your work, parts one, three, and four are ready to go. It's only parts two and five that still need work. These are the things I think we need to discuss in part two. But before we dig into them, do you have anything to add to this part?

the art of dialogue

One principle of communication and type is that it is the responsibility of the person who understands type to apply that understanding to the communication situation. When you are a team member who knows type and are working with a leader who does not verbalize the appreciation that Feeling types seek, then you can offer the recognition that may bring Feeling types on board. You can interject a statement such as the following: "I think it will help us all finish this project if we remember that we've already done good work on parts one, three, and four. It's only parts two and five that still need more work."

Jack and His Co-workers: Expressing Emotion

Jack (ENTP) is an analyst in a financial company. Barbara is a secretary. Joyce and Wendy are co-workers who try to understand Jack's responses to emotional situations.

Jack: Before we begin the meeting today, I want to acknowledge Barbara's retirement. I can't tell you how much she's meant to all of us here. This is hard. (clears throat) Barbara, we will miss you. (hands flowers to Barbara; moment of silence) Now, first on our agenda today is . . .

Wendy: (after the meeting, to Joyce) I thought Jack was going to break up when he gave those flowers to Barbara. I never expected that from him. He's always so "Let's get to business."

Joyce: And they were daisies, Barbara's favorite flowers.

Wendy: I wouldn't be surprised if he told her to order them.

Joyce: I don't think so. I think he has deep feelings about people. He just doesn't show them very often. Do you remember when Jack's brother was killed in a car crash?

Wendy: Yeah, but I didn't know much about what happened.

Joyce: As soon as Jack got the call, he pulled some of us into the break room. We were all saying he needed to just go home, but he sat there talking for almost two hours. He said he needed to wrap his mind around it before he faced his family. He said they'd expect him to be the strong one, and he had to think things through first.

Wendy: All I remember is that I waited for Jack to come out so I could say how sorry I was, and then when he did walk out, he was telling this joke about his brother, and I didn't know what to say or think.

LISTENING FOR TYPE CLUES. Jack, who has a preference for Thinking, is most comfortable and practiced with an objective approach to matters. He cares about personal relationships but is less comfortable talking about them, particularly in a business setting. When he realizes that his feelings show, he responds with analysis ("This is hard"). Then, he moves quickly to his comfort zone—the business meeting.

Jack is also uncomfortable when his Feeling function erupts in reaction to a personal tragedy. He seeks a comfort zone—in this case, co-workers in a business setting—to process his reactions, which he most likely will do through objective analysis.

APPLYING TYPE: *Thinking types and emotions.* Sometimes people have the misconception that people who prefer Thinking do not have or do not express emotions. It is important to remember that all types have emotions. Often emotions arise out of relationships with other people. Because a concern for the impact of an idea or action on other people is a natural focus for Feeling types, they frequently experience and learn to accept a rise of emotions.

People who prefer Thinking, on the other hand, first have a concern for objective principles or actions. The impact of an action or event on people is likely to be only one of many considerations that are evaluated. It is not usually the person's first area of focus. People who have a Thinking preference may find themselves surprised by sudden emotions, feel that they are out of their element, and be less practiced in dealing with the emotions. Judy Allen and Susan Brock (2000), in *Health Care and Communication Using Personality Type*, note that for Thinking types a common reaction to bad news is humor—and sometimes, dark humor. Such a reaction may also occur in response to the onslaught of sudden emotions, as illustrated in the previous story when Jack tells a joke about his brother after hearing that he had been killed.

Jocelyn and Katrina/Ryan and Sharon: Approaches to Teaching

Jocelyn (INTJ) team teaches a preschool class with Katrina who has a Feeling preference. Children seem to relate equally well to both teachers, approaching whichever one is nearest as the teachers circulate through the room. At several times during the class period, the teachers encounter similar experiences. The teachers respond to each experience in similar ways, but the wording of their responses is type related.

Jocelyn: (greeting a child who enters the room) Choose where you will go first today. Go to your first plan.

Katrina: (greeting another child) What would you like to do first today?

Jocelyn: (turning to a child who observes her tying the shoe of another child) His shoelaces need some help here.

Katrina: (to another child) Do you need help tying your shoe?

Jocelyn: (coming to the block corner) You built something tall that could crash on somebody. How could you "unbuild" it without just knocking it down?

Katrina: (later to another child in the block corner) Be careful. If it falls, it could land on your foot. That would hurt.

Jocelyn: (when a child cries and holds his finger) Show me what the problem is.

Katrina: (later, when the child cries again) Are you hurt?

Jocelyn: (to a child who leaned back on a chair and fell off) Did the chair tip over? When that happens at our house, we remind people to keep the four legs of the chair on the floor.

Katrina: (later to another child) Did you fall down? How could you sit so that won't happen to you again?

Jocelyn: (when two children want the same toy) I hear voices rising. It sounds like somebody is upset.

Katrina: (later with two other children) Do we have a problem here? How can we share the toys?

Ryan (INTJ) and Sharon (ISFJ) team teach a class of young adolescents.

Ryan: I want to show you the route you're taking to the finish of the class.

Sharon: You might want to make sure that all your prior homework assignments are in your portfolio before you turn it in.

Ryan: The leaders will have comments for you, and you will have a chance to improve the work before you meet with the people who will evaluate the portfolios.

Sharon: The evaluators want you to do well. Mostly they will say, "That's really great that you already do that work at your age." Usually, afterwards, the kids say, "That wasn't so bad."

Ryan: The evaluators will be overwhelmed at the quality of your work.

LISTENING FOR TYPE CLUES. Jocelyn and Ryan, who both have a preference for Thinking, focus on tasks, objects, and objective evaluation. Both begin class speaking about a plan or route: "Go to your first plan" and "I want to show you the route you're taking to the finish of the class." Jocelyn speaks with the children about objects: shoelaces that need help, the block tower that could crash, the hurt finger, the chair that tips over, and the rising voices. Ryan's statements involve objective evaluation: for example, "You will have a chance to improve it" and "The evaluators will be overwhelmed at the quality of your work."

Katrina and Sharon, who both have a preference for Feeling, speak in person-centered statements. For example, Katrina asks questions such as "What would you like to do?" and "Do you need help?" Sharon offers personal encouragement through statements such as "The evaluators want you to do well."

APPLYING TYPE: *Type, interests, and occupational choices.* A common misconception is that those who have a preference for Thinking do not relate to or do not have an interest in working with children. However, all types are found in and find satisfaction in any occupation.

It is true that a majority of people who choose to work with children have a Feeling preference, but many people with a Thinking preference also choose this work. The second edition of the *MBTI® Manual* (1985) reported a study of percentages of teachers at different educational levels. Among teachers at the preschool level, 21 percent reported a preference for Thinking, and 79 percent reported a preference for Feeling. At the elementary level, percentages were 32 percent for Thinking and 68 percent for Feeling. At the middle school/junior high level, percentages rose to 40 percent for Thinking and 60 percent for Feeling.

Jocelyn, who prefers Thinking, and Katrina, who prefers Feeling, use

the art of dialogue

language in subtly different ways, which is consistent with type theory. However, both are caring, interested, and effective teachers of preschool children. Ryan, who has a preference for Thinking, and Sharon, who has a preference for Feeling, also use language in ways consistent with their type differences. Still, both demonstrate concern for the adolescents and actively engage the students in positive educational experiences.

Jocelyn and Ryan: Motivation for Becoming Teachers

Jocelyn and Ryan, teachers who were introduced in the previous story, each responded to this question: What motivated your interest in child development and the education of children?

> Jocelyn: Preschool is not day care. It is early childhood education, which is social and emotional and trying to make sense of the world. I like to encourage children to do the best they can and to encourage the more intellectual things. My professional judgment is trusted, and that's a big, big thing. The preschool director is a friend and mentor. She is truly a child advocate.

> Ryan: I became convinced early on that because children are among the most vulnerable of populations, they merit effort to address their needs. I'm interested in making the class as high quality as I can. I enjoy the challenge of stimulating students to think for themselves. It provides opportunity for dialogue about issues.

LISTENING FOR TYPE CLUES. Jocelyn and Ryan both have a preference for Thinking. Both express an interest in a principle of justice for children. Jocelyn notes that the director, who is a friend and mentor, is an advocate for children. Ryan states that children, a vulnerable population, merit the effort required to address their needs. Both express concern with principles of educational quality and of fostering intellectual independence in students. Jocelyn likes to encourage intellectual endeavors and encourage children to do the best they can. Ryan wants students to think for themselves about issues. Both see teaching as a challenge to exercise professional judgment and to stimulate students.

APPLYING TYPE: *Type and gender differences.* A question among type users concerns the role of gender in the expression of type preferences. Discussions of Thinking and Feeling preferences particularly spur questions about gender differences. Perhaps this is because cultural expectations associate some characteristics related to a Thinking preference with men and some characteristics related to a Feeling preference with women. In addition, population studies of type distribution consistently indicate that more men prefer Thinking over Feeling, and more women prefer Feeling over Thinking. However, approximately 35 to 45 percent of men report a preference for Feeling, and approximately 25 to 35 percent of women report a preference for Thinking. On all other dichotomies, the distribution of the genders for any given preference is approximately the same.

A further common assumption is that men and women express type preferences differently. Based on this assumption, men who have a Thinking preference would express that preference differently than would women who have a Thinking preference. Recent studies, as well as the experiences of type users, raise questions about that assumption.

Janet Penley and Diane Stephens (1998) gathered information about parenting and type in more than 450 "Mothers of Many Styles" workshops, through research with 600 mothers, and through in-depth interviews with more than 100 mothers. The researchers compiled their findings in *The M.O.M.S.®️ Handbook*. Follow-up research indicated that at least 80 percent of the content in their book also applied to dads. Any differences between the behaviors of moms and dads seemed to be related to struggles with cultural, gender, and role expectations more than with expressions of type.

Paul Tieger and Barbara Barron-Tieger (2000) in their book *Just Your Type*, report results of studies about personality type and relationship satisfaction. Initially, they assumed that the research would need to include all possible combinations of the sixteen personality types and the two genders. For example, the authors sought the following pairs of couples:

ISTJ male, INFJ female

INFJ male, ISTJ female

Analysis of responses from couples showed so few gender differences that the researchers reported responses of any given type pairing, regardless of gender, as one result rather than two.

Children and Type

In general, the judgment function is likely to find full expression more slowly than the attitudes or the perception function. The judgment functions of

Thinking and Feeling relate to decision making, and that is a complex process. Decision-making skills involve not only type preferences but also cognitive ability, life experience, and maturity. Still, we may observe some characteristics associated with Thinking and Feeling preferences even in young children.

Brett and Liza: Characteristics of Thinking and Feeling

Brett and Liza, both four years old, are in preschool. Even at this young age, their behaviors and language suggest that they have differences in their preferences for Thinking or Feeling.

> Teacher: (to class) Let's sit on the floor in a circle for story time.
> (Brett remains in his chair studying a puzzle piece in his hand and a puzzle board on the table.)
>
> Teacher: Now, what happened to our book?
>
> Liza: You had a book when you were at the sand table. I'll show you.
>
> Teacher: Brett, wouldn't you like to hear our story?
>
> Brett: I can hear it.
>
> Liza: Here's the book. Is this the story we're going to read?
>
> Teacher: Brett, we'd like to have you in our circle.
> (Brett shakes his head. As the teacher begins reading the story, he moves his chair to sit behind Liza.)
>
> Liza: (turning around) Can you see the pictures?

LISTENING FOR TYPE CLUES. Brett and Liza are both young, and we would not want to leap to a conclusion about their types based on only one brief incident. Still, we can observe characteristics in Brett that tend to be associated with a Thinking preference. He appears to analyze the puzzle and puzzle piece. His reluctance to sit on the floor may be related to type preference as well. Thinking types, even very young children, often desire a respect for dignity. Brett may feel that sitting on the floor is undignified. He cannot be convinced otherwise.

In this scenario, Liza shows characteristics that tend to be associated with a Feeling preference. She wants to be helpful both to the teacher and to Brett.

APPLYING TYPE: *Giving affirmation.* Children often express differences between Thinking and Feeling preferences as they respond to evaluation comments a parent makes about them or their work. Elizabeth Murphy (1992) in *The Developing Child* notes that all children need affirmation, but they differ in what they accept as affirmation.

Children who have a Thinking preference need affirmation to be specific and credible. They also tend to evaluate the affirmation against their own self-assessment, which can be highly critical. For example, the parent of a Thinking child listened to his son practice a music lesson and commented, "That's good." The son responded, "No, it isn't. Why do you say that?" The father's smiling reply, "Just because," was no help, as the son showed when he said, "You don't know what it's supposed to sound like." After his next music lesson, the son told his father about a compliment from the teacher, who said the student had good breath control and tone on the high notes in a particular piece of music. The son accepted the teacher's compliment, which was specific and from a credible source.

Children who have a Feeling preference need frequent affirmation that is positive and personal. They may have doubts about their own self-assessments and depend on the opinions of others. For instance, a child with a Feeling preference was making her own greeting card for her grandmother's birthday. She showed her mother each part of her work, making comments such as, "See the pink flower I drew," "Look, I made a butterfly," and "I wrote the words in big letters." When her mother gave little response other than to look at each addition to the card, the child asked, "Don't you like my card?" The mother replied, "You know I think you draw well," to which the child answered, "But you didn't say it." The parent could have affirmed the child's need for appreciation with comments such as, "Are pink flowers your favorite color?" or "You did make big letters!" The parent could also help the child learn self-assessment skills by turning around the child's question to ask, "Do you like your card?"

Communication That Works

The two scenarios that follow demonstrate how individuals effectively adapt their communication for large-group presentations and for one-on-one meetings.

Cathy and Gary: Adapting Presentations

Cathy (ENFP) and Gary (ENTJ) are consultants who frequently give presentations

the art of dialogue

to groups. They use personality type to help them adapt their presentation approach.

> **Cathy:** Gary and I look for type clues in the body language of an audience so we can adapt our presentations based on what we see. We have a pretty standard introduction; we each do part of it.

> **Gary:** If we see a lot of smiles, nods, nudging of neighbors, then we assume many in the audience have a Feeling preference, and Cathy takes the lead for the rest of the presentation.

> **Cathy:** I have lots of examples that are likely to appeal to people who have a Feeling preference.

> **Gary:** I take a support role and add examples from a Thinking perspective.

> **Cathy:** But if most of the audience sits still and straight faced during the introduction, then Gary takes the lead for the rest of the presentation. We've learned that people who don't show much facial expression are likely to respond to Gary's examples more than mine. Of course, I still provide support and give some examples from the Feeling perspective because we know that no audience has people of only one type.

APPLYING TYPE: *Body language.* People who have a Feeling preference tend to be more expressive listeners than those with Thinking preferences, giving feedback to a speaker through body language. People who have a Thinking preference tend to give less feedback through facial expressions or body language.

Randy: Structuring Supervisory Sessions

Randy supervises unit administrators in his institution. He has recognized that the administrators are about evenly divided between those who have a preference for Thinking and those who have a preference for Feeling.

Each week Randy meets one-on-one with each administrator. When talking with those who have a preference for Thinking, he first asks for a report on the past week and whether there are any issues that need to be addressed. Sometimes he ends the supervisory session with some brief chitchat. On occasion, an administrator uses this opportunity to speak about a personal issue.

When meeting with those who have a preference for Feeling, Randy first asks about their personal lives—perhaps about their family or an activity he knows they had planned for the previous weekend. Then he moves on to discussing reports and work-related issues.

Both groups of administrators consider Randy an effective supervisor.

APPLYING TYPE: *Thinking and Feeling and personal lives.* Particularly in a work setting, people who prefer Thinking are often skeptical of the motives of a person who seems to be too interested in their personal lives. Individuals who prefer Feeling often need to know that they are appreciated as people. They do not want to feel as if they are just numbers on a payroll or cogs in an institutional wheel. One way they may perceive that they receive affirmation is through an interest in their personal lives. Note that all types need to know that any shared personal information is confidential.

When Randy structures the supervisory session in a way that fits type preferences, his administrators all feel that they are being heard. Consequently, both groups of administrators consider Randy an effective supervisor.

chapter 6 focus on the functions

"

Knowing about psychological type preferences is a useful starting point for understanding the relationship between type and communication. However, not all preferences carry equal weight in type or in communication.

As described in earlier chapters, the core of type is expressed through the four preferences that are called functions: Sensing (S), Intuition (N), Thinking (T), and Feeling (F). The content of communication is expressed through these same functions. While the attitudes or orientations of Extraversion–Introversion and Judging–Perceiving relate to how we communicate, the functions relate to what we communicate—the message itself. The whole reason we communicate is to deliver the content of a message. This is the province of the functions.

Getting the Communication Started

In chapter 1 we identified a general rule for communication—that it is the responsibility of the sender of a message to adapt to the receiver. In communication each person has a preferred starting place for receiving a message, and that starting place is related to the functions.

We can compare this communication preference to food preferences, which become apparent at a buffet restaurant where different serving areas offer different kinds of foods. Diners beginning their meal are likely to scatter among the serving areas. One goes first to the pasta and pizza buffet. Another goes first to the salad bar. A third begins at the carved meat table. Still another begins at the hot vegetable buffet. Few diners fill their plates with only one kind of food, but each has a preferred starting place.

In communication, the innate motivation for seeking the preferred content is often so strong that the receiver of a message may not even hear other information until after the person hears the desired content. During a conversation, both parties may experience frustration with communication if the sender begins first by delivering content that the receiver considers to be less important. In effective communication a sender begins a message at the preferred starting place of the receiver. The following four scenarios demonstrate the way the functions can affect communication.

> **SCENARIO 1. A physician who has a preference for Sensing may give a patient clear directions for a prescribed medication:**
>
> Take one tablet each day with a meal. Take it at the same time each day. Be sure to take it each day. Do not skip a dose, but if you miss one day, do not take two the next day. Stay with your regular dose. Before you leave today, make an appointment to come back in three months for lab tests. At that time, we will see whether the medication is helping to lower your cholesterol or whether we need to adjust the dosage. This particular drug rarely has negative interactions with your other medications, but we will do periodic checks for side effects.

If the patient has a preference for Intuition, the patient is likely to first seek information that gives the big picture: the purpose of the new medication, side effects, and long-term effects, including those on lifestyle. The patient may not hear anything else until after the physician has delivered that primary information. Then the patient may ask second-order questions such how often to take the medication, when to take it, how to take it, and so on.

In this situation, the physician may feel frustrated because the patient asks for the very information the physician has just given. The patient may also feel frustrated because the physician presented an overwhelming amount of data, data that made no sense when first presented because it was not in the context of the big picture.

> **SCENARIO 2. A teacher who has a preference for Intuition may give the following directions for a writing assignment:**
>
> The text describes three possible approaches to the issue we've discussed. Compare and contrast the appropriateness of each approach as it relates to this issue.

the art of dialogue

Typically, the student who has a Sensing preference is likely to have no idea how to begin the assignment. In fact, the student may not even hear the assignment until after receiving specific information about it: how long the paper should be; whether it's to be presented as hard copy, on a computer disk, or both; whether there are specific formatting guidelines to follow; how many and which references the student is expected to use; and what to do if the student has no actual experience with this issue.

After the student receives this specific data about the assignment, then he or she may ask questions about the content. The teacher may feel frustrated having to repeat the stated assignment and may even assume that the individual is a poor student.

SCENARIO 3. A supervisor who has a Thinking preference may outline logical reasons for employees to follow particular procedures for data input. For example, the supervisor may state the following:

Data can be analyzed quickly. Reports can be printed in a timely manner. When everyone uses the same form, anyone can quickly access needed information. If you need data from someone who is on another assignment, you can go directly to the database and finish your job without having to wait until the person on assignment is available.

The employee who has a Feeling preference may not hear the supervisor's reasoning until the supervisor reveals the personal impact of the procedure, in this case that the employee can finish the job without having to wait. At this point, the employee may ask questions about data input and analysis, the logic of the format, or accessibility of information. The supervisor may become frustrated at having to repeat information.

SCENARIO 4. A team member who has a Feeling preference may use personal testimony to persuade the team to adopt a plan. He may present statements such as the following:

"I like this approach. I've seen it work in other organizations. My friend, who works for Company X, says her whole company is enthusiastic about it."

Leaders or other team members who have a preference for Thinking may first need to hear logical reasons why the plan is appropriate for this company before they can focus on the team member's testimonials and the experience of other companies.

Each of these scenarios illustrates the power of the functions to affect communication. Awareness of type along with careful observation and listening for preferred functions can help individuals hypothesize likely starting points for communication.

Function Pairs in Action

ST	SF	NF	NT
Sensing and Thinking	Sensing and Feeling	Intuition and Feeling	Intuition and Thinking

One way to look at content is through function pairs, which are the two middle letters of a type code: ST, SF, NF, and NT. This approach simplifies the process of adapting communication to psychological type because it looks at only four sets of characteristics for function pairs rather than at eight preferences or sixteen types. Table 6.1 (76–77) provides descriptions of the four function pairs.

Susan Brock (1991) observed the importance of function pairs as she developed Flex Talk® to apply personality type in communication. She asked several hundred people who knew their type preferences how they preferred to be influenced in leadership, teamwork, managing, sales, and other similar situations. She later asked similar questions about communication in health-care situations. While Brock found that each type preference contributes in some way to communication, she discovered that the heart of the communication process involves the function pairs—ST, SF, NF, NT.

Stories that illustrate function pairs in action follow. As in the earlier stories related to preferences, communication reveals clues to psychological type through the speaker's focus of interest and use of words that are characteristic of particular preferences.

ST–NF: Adapting a Financial Statement

ST	SF	NF	NT
Sensing and Thinking	Sensing and Feeling	**Intuition and Feeling**	Intuition and Thinking

Some forms of communication, such as a financial statement, seem so standard that people may not even think about adapting them to type preferences. Typically, a financial report such as that shown in figure 6.1 tends to be written from a perspective of Sensing and Thinking (ST). As such, it is brief, states just the facts, and uses accounting terminology.

figure 6.1
ST Financial Statement

NET REVENUES .... **$xxx.xx**
EXPENSES:
    Personnel .... xxx.xx
    Supplies, support services .... xxx.xx
    Depreciation .... xxx.xx
    Interest expense .... xxx.xx
Total expenses .... **xxx.xx**
NET INCOME .... **xxx.xx**

The staff of a private hospital knew that the majority of its personnel, directors, and financial supporters had preferences for Intuition and Feeling (NF). Consequently, those responsible for the financial statement adapted the standard format to accommodate the NF type preferences. What resulted is presented in figure 6.2.

figure 6.2
NF Financial Statement

REVENUES

We billed patients for—Room, board and general services . . $xxx.xx

But because of required contractual and other allowances,
and the inability of patients to pay in full, we charged off . . (xxx.xx)

Therefore, our net revenues from patient services were .... xxx.xx

In addition, we received—
    State aid .... xxx.xx
    Grants .... xxx.xx

Therefore, our total operating revenues were .... **$xxx.xx**

OPERATING EXPENSES

We paid—Salaries, wages, and employee benefits .... $xxx.xx

Supplies, support services, and depreciation .... xxx.xx

Interest expense .... xxx.xx

Total operating expenses .... **xxx.xx**

EXCESS OF REVENUES OVER EXPENSES .... **$xxx.xx**

table 6.1
Characteristics of Function Pairs

People Who Prefer Sensing and Thinking (ST) Function Pair	People Who Prefer Sensing and Feeling (SF) Function Pair
Tend to want others to know that they	**Tend to want others to know that they**
• are interested in efficient, practical, sensible approaches • value real-life experience	• provide warm, personal, practical support to others • value personal loyalty
In communication, tend to	**In communication, tend to**
• want to simplify experience and focus on essentials with unambiguous facts • want short businesslike interactions • want time to absorb information	• want general rules that help them validate experience in personal and practical ways • want orderly uncomplicated processes • want complete information
In interpersonal relationships, may	**In interpersonal relationships, may**
• want roles defined in specific and objective ways • build trust through seeing accurate facts and responsible actions	• be concerned with everyday matters related to self and others • build trust through establishing and maintaining personal relationships
Others often observe that they may	**Others often observe that they may**
• make brief statements • make logical comparisons between facts • seek third-party opinions only if they see the information as relevant and can actually contact the third party • use and want to hear straightforward language • expect efficient attention to details • use impersonal words ("the problem")	• tell stories from a personal viewpoint • ask others about personal experiences • seek third-party opinions if they see the third party as being like themselves • use and want to hear factual but sensitive language • expect others to give their complete attention and remember what has already been said • use personal words ("our problem")
Others may be put off because they	**Others may be put off because they**
• often seem immediately opposed to new ideas or change • tend to be impatient with or uninterested in others' viewpoints • often seem too strict in their interpretation of rules	• often seem immediately afraid of new ideas or change • tend to be focused on other people to the extent that they seem meddlesome, or perpetual worriers or neglectful of their own needs • often seem to bend rules too quickly

the art of dialogue

table 6.1 *continued*
Characteristics of Function Pairs

People Who Prefer Intuition and Feeling (NF) Function Pair	People Who Prefer Intuition and Thinking (NT) Function Pair
Tend to want others to know that they	**Tend to want others to know that they**
• value making a difference in the world • want to be treated as a unique individual	• seek to understand and have a rationale for everything • value independence and competency in self and others
In communication, they tend to	**In communication, they tend to**
• use stream of consciousness thinking to find essentials in ambiguities or subtleties • appear prophetic by imagining potential outcomes • want to be involved in choosing among alternatives	• be interested in intriguing possibilities that are tested against principles • avoid surprises by anticipating potential problems • want straightforward information with reasonable alternatives
In interpersonal relationships, they may	**In interpersonal relationships, they may**
• assume competency exists • want others to appreciate them as a person rather than as a number or case	• assume appreciation is understood • confirm confidence in self or others through increased responsibilities or new challenges
Others often observe that they may	**Others often observe that they may**
• create a word picture of an image or feeling • use and look for body language • seek to synthesize ideas into a harmonious whole • brainstorm possibilities such as "This could make a difference because . . ." or "An alternative could be . . ." • speak diplomatically; or criticize passionately if values are violated	• create models or strategies to summarize theoretical ideas • appear aloof • check for discrepancies in information or sources • show interest by testing knowledge and competency of others; ask "What are the down sides?" or "What will you do if . . . ?" • use dark humor or barbed wit, especially to mask emotions
Others may be put off because they	**Others may be put off because they**
• often seem to avoid getting down to business • may appear too accommodating at first, then inflexible	• often seem blunt, critical, and argumentative • may appear to be unaware of discord

LISTENING FOR TYPE CLUES. The hospital statement includes personal and everyday language such as "we billed" and "we charged off," and "our net revenues were." It also contains explanatory words and phrases rather than technical accounting terms: "because of the inability of patients to pay in full" and "excess of revenues over expenses." Such language describes concepts (Intuition) more than facts (Sensing). It is person-centered (Feeling), using words such as "we" and "our." Characteristics associated with the NF function pair include a focus on concepts that impact the people who are involved.

SF–NF: Pleasing Others

ST	SF	NF	NT
Sensing and Thinking	**Sensing and Feeling**	**Intuition and Feeling**	Intuition and Thinking

Linda (ISFJ) and Hattie (ESFP) are widowed sisters who live together. Several times a year they host their niece Melissa (ENFP) for overnight visits. Both of the aunts and their niece value harmony in their relationship with each other and take special steps to preserve that harmony. Because of their differences in Sensing and Intuition, they seek to support the relationship in different ways.

Linda: What shall we have for breakfast? We need something special for Melissa.

Hattie: What about banana pancakes? If I remember right, Melissa likes those. Don't you, Melissa?

Linda: Oh, that would be a special treat.

Hattie: I bought blueberry syrup. I remember that you like blueberry syrup, Melissa.

Linda: And I think I remember that you like pecans in your banana pancakes, but you don't like walnuts. Just pecans.

Hattie: Well, then, let's try pecans. That would be extra special.

Melissa: (later, to a friend) It's really kind of funny. Every time I visit them, Aunt Linda and Aunt Hattie have the same conversation about breakfast and serve the same thing, but it's always like they just had a brand new idea. I don't know where they get the idea I like blueberry syrup. I really don't like it, but they make a special trip to the supermarket to buy it just for me. Maybe someone else who visits them likes blueberry syrup. They invite so many guests, and they always try to please each one. I don't want to hurt their feelings, so I just eat it and pretend I like it.

LISTENING FOR TYPE CLUES. Linda and Hattie both have preferences for Sensing and Feeling, the SF function pair. Using their Sensing function, they pay attention to and remember details—accurately most of the time. With their Feeling function, they care for and about other people. The combination of Sensing and Feeling (SF) leads them to focus on details about people, especially the many people who are important to them.

Melissa has preferences for Intuition and Feeling, the NF function pair. With her Feeling function, she also cares about other people and doesn't want to hurt their feelings. When Linda and Hattie make a mistake about what she likes, Melissa uses her Intuition to think of possible reasons to excuse the mistake. The combination of Intuition and Feeling (NF) leads her to generate possibilities that can help preserve harmony in the relationship between herself and her aunts.

NT: Competency with a Precise Vocabulary

ST	SF	NF	**NT**
Sensing and Thinking	Sensing and Feeling	Intuition and Feeling	**Intuition and Thinking**

Tanner teaches a graduate-level seminar in developmental psychology. In these excerpts from a class discussion, he exhibits NT characteristics. As you listen for type-related clues, notice particularly Tanner's choice of words.

Tanner: I was pleased with the proposals for your papers. It's important to me that you're able to provide a focused critique on a topic in depth. (turning, with a smile, to one student) I have great respect for your audacity to critique a paper I wrote. Your points were on target.

What's important about developmental transitions is how they're interpreted. This is the first time we've talked about individual differences being paramount over normative predictions we can make.

The degree to which there is "dis-synchronicity" between kids' expectations and parents' expectations is culturally relative. Does this seem like a reasonable argument?

LISTENING FOR TYPE CLUES. Though we have only a few statements from Tanner, we can hypothesize that he has preferences for Intuition and Thinking. He values competency in students—the ability to provide a focused, in-depth critique on a topic. He has a dry humor and respects intelligence: a student aptly critiques the instructor's paper. Tanner is interested in theories of developmental psychology and wants students to test the principles in the theories. He easily uses precise terms to convey the nuances and full meaning of his thoughts. These behaviors are characteristics of someone with a combination of the Intuition and Thinking functions.

APPLYING TYPE: *Using precise words.* People who have a preference for Intuition and Thinking (NT) often have large vocabularies from which to choose words that convey precise meaning. In the drive for precision, NT speakers may even coin new terms just as Tanner coined "dis-synchronicity." Further discussion on the precise use of vocabulary is included in chapter 13.

A historical example of coining terms comes from Carl Jung, who had NT preferences and who developed the theory of psychological types that is the basis of the MBTI® theory and instrument. Jung coined the terms *extraversion* and *introversion* from Latin root words that mean "outward-turning" and "inward-turning." Other people, however, do not always recognize and use words with the same precision originally intended by an NT speaker. As Jung's terms became part of the common American vocabulary, the words lost the precision of their original meaning. People who are interested in the theory of psychological type find that they must reclaim the original NT precision of Jung's terms *extraversion* and *introversion* to understand the characteristics of the preferences.

NT–NF: The Missing Pieces

Dylan (INTJ) is director of training for a company in the service sector. His primary focus is training for in-house staff. Mason (INTP) is assistant director. His primary focus is training for field representatives. Melanie (INFJ) is administrative assistant for the training department.

the art of dialogue

As you listen to Melanie describe office interactions and the frustration that she feels, watch for ways in which Dylan and Mason live out their NT preferences. Watch for skills the team needs to do their work that do not come naturally to them. Listen for the impact of the missing pieces in the frustration you hear in Melanie's voice.

> **Melanie:** Dylan and Mason are both nice guys and good trainers, but sometimes they're like two ships passing in the night. I'm the one who's supposed to keep them from colliding.
>
> Little things come up all the time. The latest was that they both scheduled training on our new service product for the same place at the same time. Nicki in tech support discovered it. She's a detail person who gets equipment ready for training. She's often my eyes and ears.
>
> It turns out Mason had checked calendars with all the field reps. Dylan had checked calendars with accounting and HR, but Mason and Dylan didn't check with each other. And, as usual, they forgot to schedule the room with me. It took me two full days to reschedule everything, as if I didn't already have enough to do.
>
> Then the guys gave me their materials to reproduce. It's not my job to edit, but I happened to notice differences in their flow charts showing who was responsible for what. They weren't big differences, but enough to create confusion among staff and frustration for customers.
>
> Sometimes I'd like to grab them both by the scruff of the neck, lock them in an empty room, and tell them they can't come out until they talk to each other.

LISTENING FOR TYPE CLUES. Dylan and Mason both have preferences for Intuition and Thinking (NT). They focus conceptually on systems but appear to miss details that would make their systems practical and usable. Melanie also sees them as oblivious to the impact of their actions on other people.

Melanie, who has preferences for Intuition and Feeling (NF), also has a conceptual perspective, but her focus is on people. She understands how overlooking details affects her bosses, the staff, customers, and herself.

APPLYING TYPE: *Type is not an excuse.* Dylan, Mason, and Melanie all have preferences for Introversion, but this preference does not explain or excuse the apparent lack of communication among them. It may, however, influence the preferred medium of communication.

None of them, for example, may be comfortable with extended conversations. They may prefer to communicate through notes, e-mails, and short, focused meetings.

Further, none of the team members has a preference for Sensing. Nevertheless, the job requires some attention to details. Melanie (NF) appears to have developed skill using her less-preferred Sensing function and notices other people in the organization who have the Sensing preference or skills in using the function.

All people and teams sometimes need to use skills associated with less-preferred functions. There are two ways to develop such skills, and Melanie appears to successfully use both of them:

1) Purposeful practice
2) Working with and consulting with others who have those particular preferences.

APPLYING TYPE: *Leadership.* Neither Dylan nor Mason has a preference for Feeling or Sensing, and both combine the Thinking preference with Intuition (NT). A leadership strength of people who have NT preferences is that they tend to foster independence. They trust that colleagues are knowledgeable and competent in their jobs. Leaders who have NT preferences tend to assume that colleagues will come to them with any questions or problems that may arise.

Dylan and Mason appear to lead almost entirely from the NT functions. They follow their tendency to foster independence to such an extent that they do not dialogue with each other. They trust the knowledge and competency of colleagues and staff to such an extent that they fail to check in with Melanie. Both apparently ignore needed skills associated with their less-preferred Sensing and Feeling functions. They seem to be unaware of missed or conflicting details that are necessary to make their ideas workable. They seem oblivious to the impact of their decisions and actions on other people. Dylan and Mason do not recognize that they create confusion among staff and frustration for customers when they operate almost exclusively from their preferred NT functions.

Because Dylan and Mason do not exhibit skills in the use of their less-preferred Sensing and Feeling preferences, they would be more effective if they asked for and listened to a co-worker's perspective—in this case, Melanie's. Such adaptations would help to keep communication open within the team and the organization.

the art of dialogue

The story of Dylan and Mason illustrates strengths and pitfalls of NT leadership characteristics. However, each type has its own set of strengths and corresponding weaknesses. When a leader of any type overuses the strengths of that type, the result is likely to be a corresponding exaggeration of the leader's weaknesses, as well as lack of communication within the team or organization. To enhance effectiveness, leaders can take the following steps:

- Listen to team members to identify things they may otherwise miss in their natural work and communication patterns;
- Include extra uninterrupted time for tasks that require use of less-preferred functions, particularly if that time is scheduled at a point in the day when they have more energy and are less tired and stressed;
- Consult with colleagues or supervisors who have skills they lack;
- Empower team members who have skills they lack;
- Seek mentors who can help them learn and practice needed skills associated with less-preferred functions;
- Adopt teamwork strategies that maximize the contributions of all psychological type preferences.

The Z Pattern

A simple problem-solving strategy, called the Z pattern, can minimize the risk of overuse of strengths and foster communication. The Z pattern includes four steps that incorporate the use of Sensing, Intuition, Thinking, and Feeling—the four preferences that make up the function pairs. The term Z pattern refers to the order for using the functions in problem solving, as shown in figure 6.3 (page 84). The two perception (information-gathering) functions of Sensing and Intuition appear on the first line. The two judgment (decision-making) functions of Thinking and Feeling appear on the second line. When the functions are connected in order, the result looks like a Z.

The steps of the Z pattern use the four functions to examine the facts, generate possibilities, analyze consequences, and consider the impact on people. The series of questions included with the four steps can help you put each step into practice. Make a decision only after you have taken all four steps. For effective implementation, repeat the Z pattern with each piece of the implementation.

figure 6.3
Z Pattern: A Decision-Making Strategy

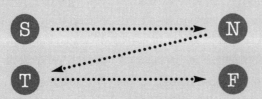

1) **Use the Sensing function to consider facts**. Pay attention to the who, what, when, and where of an idea The main question to ask at this stage is "What is?"
   a) What is the issue, problem, or definition?
   b) What is the purpose or goal?
   c) What is the time frame?
   d) What is the status of resources?
      ◦ financial resources?
      ◦ physical space, if applicable?
      ◦ equipment and supplies, if applicable?
      ◦ people resources?

2) **Use the Intuition function to generate as many possibilities as you can.** The question to ask here relates to "What could be?"
   a) What are the ideas?
   b) What are the possibilities?
   c) What is the vision?
   d) What are the dreams?
   e) What might the ideals be?

3) **Use the Thinking function to analyze the likely consequences of each proposed idea or action.** The question to ask here relates to "What would be the consequences if . . .?"
   a) What would be the benefits if this possibility were enacted?
   b) What would be the disadvantages?
   c) What would the effect be on the goal, financial resources, physical space, and so on?
   d) What would the short-term consequences be to the larger organization?
   e) What would the long-term consequences be?

4) **Use the Feeling function to consider the likely effect of each proposed idea or action on people.** The question to ask here has two parts, each beginning "How would the idea or action affect . . .?"
   a) How would the idea or action affect people?
      ◦ Who would be affected? (for example, staff? customers? clients? students?)
      ◦ In what ways would each person be affected?
   b) How would the idea or action affect values?
      ◦ How would this support the values of the individual, group, or organization?
      ◦ How would this undermine the values?

the art of dialogue

The Z pattern can be a useful problem-solving strategy both for individuals and for teams. In both situations, the Z pattern provides a way to give attention to all four functions, ensuring that no function is completely ignored. In teams, use of the Z pattern can foster communication. However, for the Z pattern to be an effective problem-solving strategy, the team leader also needs to create a climate that encourages communication. Especially important is giving voice to those team members who bring the perspective of underrepresented functions. This course of action sometimes means that the leader and team agree that minority viewpoints count and that they may even receive additional weight to achieve the goal of using all four functions in the problem-solving process.

Children and Type

ST	SF	NF	NT
Sensing and Thinking	**Sensing and Feeling**	Intuition and Feeling	**Intuition and Thinking**

Students and teachers may find communication difficult when they differ in their type preferences. Some teachers who know type do help ease difficulties by adapting their communication and teaching methods to meet the needs of students who have different type preferences. Still, students also need to adapt to teachers' methods of communication and teaching, even though the students are young and have immature type development.

In the following story, a fifth-grade student has problems in school. The student has preferences for Intuition and Thinking. According to an analysis of type preferences of teachers at different levels of education (*MBTI® Manual*, 1985), the most common function pair among elementary teachers is Sensing and Feeling (SF). A student who has Intuition and Thinking (NT) preferences is likely to have few, if any, teachers of his type in elementary school. He may not even encounter many teachers of his type until he reaches the university level.

The counselor in the story recognizes and accepts typical characteristics of the student's type preferences. The counselor does not try to talk the student out of his preferences nor out of his reaction to the different preferences of the teacher. Instead the counselor proposes a plan to help the student adapt to the teacher's type preferences.

NT: Josh and His Counselor

Josh, a fifth-grade student, didn't like school. His teacher didn't like the quality of his work, and his mother was displeased with his low grades. All agreed Josh knew more than he demonstrated. When Josh turned in a half page of work after being assigned a two-page essay, he was sent to a counselor.

The counselor administered the *Murphy-Meisgeier Type Indicator for Children*™ assessment. After interpretation of the results, Josh verified preferences for Intuition and Thinking (NT). The counselor was aware that Josh's teacher had preferences for Sensing and Feeling (SF). After discussing with Josh differences between his type preferences and other preferences, the counselor turned attention to the essay.

Counselor: When your teacher sees this paper, it probably looks to her like an outline rather than an essay.

Josh: I don't know what else to say. I said everything I know.

Counselor: Let's look at the first sentence. When you wrote it, you knew all the things that sentence means. But your teacher only knows what you wrote in the sentence. She doesn't know all the other things you mean.

Josh: Then she's stupid.

Counselor: Maybe it seems to you that your teacher isn't as smart as you. Maybe you'll just have to become a teacher for your teacher. Try this. After you write a sentence, write everything the sentence means. Tell your teacher all the things you think she doesn't know.

Josh: That's dumb.

Josh thought the counselor's advice was dumb, but Josh did what the counselor said. His explanations filled the two pages of paper. Overall, his grades went up, and his mother was pleased. According to Josh, his mother and teacher quit getting on his case when he did the "dumb" work of explaining what they were too stupid to understand.

 APPLYING TYPE: *NT and communication.* Thinking types tend to value efficiency and brevity. They often dislike repetition, as it seems like a waste of time and energy. Those who combine Thinking

the art of dialogue

with Intuition may have large vocabularies that allow them to communicate with efficiency and economy of language. They can choose words that convey precise meanings. They may speak in terse statements about broad principles, assuming that all the details and consequences are implicit. Sometimes they are unaware that others may view their written work as outlines rather than finished pieces.

Children who have NT preferences often do not have teachers who understand their communication mode. Josh's counselor, however, recognized his frustration at not being understood. By verbalizing to Josh his perspective of the situation, the counselor created a climate to help Josh accept a suggestion for coping with the frustration he, his mother, and his teacher felt. The suggestion helped Josh put down on paper what he assumed he had said.

Communication That Works

ST	SF	NF	NT
Sensing and Thinking	Sensing and Feeling	**Intuition and Feeling**	Intuition and Thinking

Doug's father was dying. Doug had preferences for Intuition and Feeling (NF), as did most of the other family members who had gathered in the hospital waiting room. They agreed that Dad was agitated and had issues he needed to talk about. One by one they went to Dad's bedside, speaking to him from the natural language of their own NF preferences with phrases such as these:

"How do you feel, Dad?"

"Dad, I feel we need to talk."

"It's OK to feel scared."

"It would help you feel better, Dad, if you would talk about it."

Dad remained stoic, silent, and restless. Then Doug shared an insight with family members, most of whom knew a bit about psychological type. "We've been using the word feel, but we all know that Dad probably has a preference for Thinking," Doug explained.

Doug returned to the hospital room.

"Dad, how do you think things are going?" Doug asked.

"Not so good. I'm worried about Mama. All our married life I've tried to do my best to take care of her. I've got insurance and my retirement and some other savings. I thought I was taking care of her, but I don't know if she knows what all is there or how to get it. (Dad began to cry.) How will Mama be taken care of when I'm gone?"

Doug said "Can we think together about what you have and where it is? I'll make a list and take care of it."

Over the next several hours, Doug's father talked about financial matters, then maintenance on the house and car, and finally his thoughts about life and death. Then he drifted into a peaceful sleep and died that night.

LISTENING FOR TYPE CLUES. Doug and other family members asked questions from their own preferences for Intuition and Feeling (NF). Characteristic of people with the NF function pair, they wanted to talk first about philosophical and personal thoughts on life and death.

When Doug asked his dad a different question, he opened a way for his father to answer with an objective report, almost as if his father were analyzing someone else's situation. This approach allowed Doug's father to talk first about practical concerns, an indication that the father likely had a preference for Sensing, as well as the previously recognized Thinking preference. After Doug's father spoke from his Sensing and Thinking (ST) preferences, he then began to talk about life and death from the perspective of his less-preferred functions, Intuition and Feeling. Although he could not start talking from these preferences, as demonstrated by his initial lack of response to efforts to communicate, he was able to talk about philosophical issues after handling the practical issues.

APPLYING TYPE: *Simple adaptation.* Adapting language can be as simple as changing a few words, or even a single word. Doug's father began to talk when Doug changed the question from "How do you feel?" to "How do you think things are going?"

Summing Up Use of Preferences and Function Pairs in Communication

When we listen for type clues in preferences and function pairs, we can enhance communication by adapting to another person's mode. Sometimes we hear clues to the preferences of Extraversion or Introversion, or Judging or Perceiving, and we get hints as to *how* another person prefers to give or receive a message. When we hear clues to the preferences of Sensing or Intuition, or Thinking or Feeling, we get hints about *what* the person considers most important in the message.

the art of dialogue

Sometimes we hear clues to the function pairs of Sensing and Thinking (ST), Sensing and Feeling (SF), Intuition and Feeling (NF), or Intuition and Thinking (NT). The function pairs can help us focus on the content of the message, as well as simplify the process of adapting communication to psychological types. With function pairs, we look at four sets of functions rather than at eight preferences or sixteen types. Function pairs also help us recognize the interaction of the preferences. For example, we see differences between ST and SF characteristics, or between ST and NT characteristics.

While looking at four sets of characteristics helps us simplify our approach to communication, looking at the interactions of preferences in the function pairs helps us avoid becoming simplistic in our approach. In the next section of this book, we deepen our knowledge of the interaction of preferences through an understanding of type dynamics.

3

part three **type dynamics**

As discussed in part 2, understanding each preference in a psychological type code as well as function pairs is critical in enhancing communication. However, psychological type is more than adding together four sets of characteristics. Each preference interacts with each of the others in a dynamic, not static, way so that the whole is greater than the sum of its parts. Type dynamics reveals these interactions and the order of importance of each preference for each of the sixteen types. Overall, type dynamics leads to a deeper level of understanding of both psychological type and communication.

Part 3 of this book explains the fundamental principles of type dynamics and the implications for communication.

"The eight dimensions of psychological type provide just a flat snapshot of the mental processes. Type dynamics, however, is the three-dimensional version."

Roger R. Pearman and Sarah C. Albritton,
I'm Not Crazy, I'm Just Not You

chapter 7 the basics of type dynamics

Type dynamics is a theory that explains the complex interactions of psychological type preferences. Each preference in a type code interacts with every other preference to create a dynamic whole.

Premise of Type Dynamics Theory

Type dynamics theory emphasizes that each of the sixteen personality types is a dynamic whole. To help users grasp an understanding of psychological type, writers and trainers tend to break down type into parts—individual preferences, preference combinations, Extraverted and Introverted attitudes of functions, and so on. However, whole type is more than the sum of the pieces. Each preference in a psychological type code interacts with each of the other preferences.

Whole Type

In short conversations, clues to individual type preferences generally are more apparent than clues to a whole type. The following story, however, provides an example of the interactions of preferences in a whole type.

Josie (ESFP) answered the telephone.

Caller: What are you doing?

Josie: I just got home. I cleaned house this morning, took Aunt Mary to do some shopping, went and cleaned Doris's house—she's not feeling well—then went to the rehabilitation center to stay with Florence because Leslie had to go to the city today, so Florence was alone, and I stayed while we watched the ballgame, and I've been here about ten minutes, so I'm sitting in front of the TV relaxing.

LISTENING FOR TYPE CLUES. Josie begins the conversation by speaking from Sensing, giving all the details of her day. The details center on her concern and care for people who are important to her, an expression of the Feeling function. Sensing and Feeling are the two middle letters of Josie's ESFP type code. They are the core of the type and represent *what* concerns her. These functions are the source of the content of Josie's message.

The attitudes of Extraversion and Perceiving reflect *how* Josie uses her core functions. Josie tells all the details of her day in one sentence—a common communication characteristic of those who have a preference for Extraversion. In the interaction of the preferences, the content of the message reveals clues to the Extraversion preference. The Sensing details are more about activities than about reflection on facts or data. The expression of concern for people (Feeling) is also action oriented.

Josie also has a preference for Perceiving. It is unlikely that she planned to do all of the activities that she actually did that day. She simply moved into each one as it arose. On the other hand, it is also unlikely that the activities Josie described were the only possible options that presented themselves during the day, nor the only things she did or thought during the day. While she probably moved spontaneously through the day, she moved toward or away from options based on the influence of her Sensing, Feeling, and Extraversion preferences. At the end of the day, all of the preferences influenced what she described or did not describe when she was asked about her day.

While Josie exhibited characteristics of each of the preferences of her type in her activities and conversation, she also revealed the interactions of the preferences in the whole type.

Two Basic Concepts of Type Dynamics

The emphasis in type dynamics is on the core of the personality. The concepts of balance and hierarchical order of functions describe the operation of the type core, which consists of the four functions: Sensing (S), Intuition (N), Thinking

94

(T), and Feeling (F). These functions reflect two fundamental mental processes: perception and judgment. Perception is the process of gathering information through Sensing or Intuition. Judgment is the process of making decisions though Thinking or Feeling.

Attitude/orientation	Extraversion–Introversion	How
Perception function	Sensing–Intuition	What
Judgment function	Thinking–Feeling	What
Attitude/orientation	Judging–Perceiving	How

Balance

Balance is a key concept of type dynamics, and the word *balance* has a specific definition in psychological type theory. *Balance* refers to a lead role for one preference, process, or attitude, with a supporting and complementary (not competitive) role for an opposite preference, process, or attitude. Note that *balance* does *not* mean "equality."

Fundamental processes and balance. In type dynamics, one of the fundamental processes—perception or judgment—plays a lead role and the other plays a supporting role. This interaction provides balance in the personality type so that each person has a preferred way of gathering information as well as a preferred way of making decisions about the information. Which one of the two named functions takes the lead and which plays the supporting role is specific to each of the sixteen types. Further discussion on this dynamic follows later in the chapter.

Extraversion–Introversion and balance. The attitudes of Extraversion and Introversion, represented in the first letter of the type code impact the direction and use of the functions and also have a role in the concept of balance. The first letter identifies the preferred direction of energy and the focus of attention of the lead function in the type. If a person has a preference for Extraversion, the person uses the lead function in the outer world. If a person has a preference for Introversion, the person uses the lead function in the inner world.

The supporting function is used in the opposite attitude. Consequently, if a person uses a lead function in an Extraverted way, then that person uses the supporting function in an Introverted way, and vice versa. In this manner the attitudes as well as the functions provide balance in the personality.

Balance, then, includes two things:

- balance between perception (information gathering) and judgment (decision making)
- balance between Extraversion for one function in the type and Introversion for the other function identified in the type code.

Balance in operation. Trainers may see this concept of balance in operation as they observe participants over several days of training. Early in the training, people who have a preference for Extraversion may ask lots of questions and offer lots of examples. They may say, "Let me see if I understand" and repeat or restate what the trainer has just said. Later, they may be quiet, even if the trainer asks questions or offers opportunities for volunteers to summarize or demonstrate the learning of the training. People who have a preference for Introversion are more likely to listen quietly early in the training. Later, they may answer questions and volunteer to review material or demonstrate learning.

When looking solely at preferences, we observe that Extraverts prefer to learn by thinking aloud while Introverts prefer to learn through reflection. Through the lens of type dynamics, however, we observe the concept of balance at work. Extraverts begin the learning through their Extraverted function. Then they integrate the learning through their Introverted function. Introverts begin the learning through their Introverted function. Then they integrate the learning through their Extraverted function. Each group, then, demonstrates the concept of balance through the use of an Extraverted function and an Introverted function. A preference for Extraversion or for Introversion influences the order in which the person uses the Extraverted and Introverted functions.

The Hierarchy of the Functions

The concept of the hierarchy of the functions is that each of the sixteen psychological types uses the functions of Sensing, Intuition, Thinking, and Feeling in a particular order. One of the two functions identified in the second and third letters of a type code plays the lead role in any given psychological type. This function is commonly called the dominant function. The other function identified in the type code takes a supporting role and is called the auxiliary function.

The two alternative functions that are not identified in the type code also contribute to the personality type. These too have an order and are called the third (or tertiary) function, and the fourth (or least-preferred) function.

We can and do use all four functions, although we have a natural preference for one perception function and one judgment function. When we have well-developed use of type, we draw on the unnamed and less-preferred functions as appropriate and needed.

The dominant function. The lead function among Sensing, Intuition, Thinking, or Feeling is called the dominant function. There are many descriptions for the dominant function—captain of the ship, guiding star, lead actor, motivating factor, and unifying force of the personality. According to type development theory, the dominant function is the first one to find expression in childhood. A person usually comes to rely on the dominant function, to develop skill with it, and to trust it. A person uses the dominant function in his or her preferred world. Thus, a person who prefers Extraversion uses the dominant function in an Extraverted way. A person who prefers Introversion uses the dominant function in an Introverted way.

The auxiliary function. We can think of the auxiliary, or supporting, function as the first mate, the general's aide, the supporting actor, or the complement. According to type development theory, it is the second function to develop, usually in adolescence.

The auxiliary function provides balance in two ways.

- **It is the opposite fundamental process from the dominant function.** If the dominant function is a perception function (Sensing or Intuition), then the auxiliary function is a judgment function (Thinking or Feeling). If the dominant function is a judgment function (Thinking or Feeling), then the auxiliary function is a perception function (Sensing or Intuition).
- **It operates in the opposite attitude from the dominant process.** If the dominant function is Extraverted, then the auxiliary function is Introverted. If the dominant function is Introverted, then the auxiliary function is Extraverted.

The third function. The third, or tertiary, function—which is not named in the type code—plays a minor, supporting role in type dynamics. According to type development theory, the third function finds expression later in life, after the dominant and auxiliary functions have developed.

The third function is always the opposite preference on the same dichotomy as the auxiliary function.

- If the auxiliary function is Sensing (one of the perception functions), then the third function is Intuition; if the auxiliary function is Intuition, then the third function is Sensing.

- If the auxiliary function is Thinking (one of the judgment functions), then the third function is Feeling; if the auxiliary function is Feeling, then the third function is Thinking.

Type theorists have proposed three different theories about the attitude of the third function. One theory states that the third function has the opposite attitude of the dominant function and the same attitude as the auxiliary and fourth functions. For example, if the dominant function is Extraverted, then the third function is Introverted. The hypothesis underlying this theory is that the dominant function is such a powerful force in the personality that all three of the other functions must be in the opposite attitude to achieve balance.

A second theory is that the attitude of the third function is the same as the attitude of the dominant function and opposite of the attitude of the auxiliary and fourth functions. The hypothesis underlying this theory is that the personality achieves balance because the perception and judgment functions each have one Extraverted and one Introverted function.

A third theory states that the third function can be either Extraverted or Introverted. The hypothesis underlying this theory is that the third function is the most flexible of all the functions in its attitude. It most easily adapts attitude to what is needed in a given situation. Table 7.1 summarizes the three theories. Note that because these three different theories about the attitude of the third function exist, no attitude is assigned to it in this book.

table 7.1
Attitude of the Third Function

Theory 1			Theory 2			Theory 3		
Dominant	E	I	Dominant	E	I	Dominant	E	I
Auxiliary	I	E	Auxiliary	I	E	Auxiliary	I	E
Third	I	E	Third	E	I	Third	I/E	E/I
Fourth	I	E	Fourth	I	E	Fourth	I	E

The fourth function. The fourth function is also referred to as the least-preferred function, the least-developed function, and the inferior function. Some people make a distinction in these terms, associating the first three with purposeful, conscious use of the function and the latter, inferior function with its more unconscious expression.

The terms *fourth function, least-preferred function,* and *least-developed function* reflect the idea that even when we use this function in a purposeful,

98

conscious way, it is the most difficult and most energy draining to use. In fact, if we procrastinate it is likely to be on something that requires use of this least-preferred fourth function. Further, even when using it appropriately, we typically use it in a less skilled way.

The term *inferior function* is most descriptive when the fourth function erupts from somewhere in the personality that seems to be beyond conscious control. This term describes the function when we don't act like ourselves. Sometimes people describe the inferior function as putting a foot in the mouth. When the fourth function suddenly takes control, our words or actions may signal that we are experiencing stress, fatigue, or illness, or are in some other way not ourselves.

The fourth function comes from the same dichotomy as the dominant function.

- If the dominant function is Sensing or Intuition (a perception function), then the fourth function is the opposite preference in that dichotomy.

- If the dominant function is Thinking or Feeling (a judgment function), then the fourth function is the opposite preference in that dichotomy.

The attitude of the fourth function is opposite the attitude of the dominant function.

- If the dominant function is Extraverted, then the fourth function is Introverted.

- If the dominant function is Introverted, then the fourth function is Extraverted.

During a spurt of type development, a person can become quite interested in skills associated with the function being developed at that time. However, although development may focus on the third or fourth function, that function usually remains less comfortable to use and less accessible than the dominant and auxiliary functions. In the handedness exercise described in chapter 1 of this book, we noted that sometimes a person finds it an interesting challenge to write his or her name with the less-preferred hand. However, if that person had to take lecture notes that way, he or she would likely be frustrated and quite possibly ready to give up the task. This reaction also describes the typical experience of someone using the third or fourth function.

The Role of Judging and Perceiving Preferences

The last letter of the type code—J (Judging) or P Perceiving—identifies which fundamental process is Extraverted. It identifies the process that is used in the outer world, the process others are most likely to see first in us.

- If a person prefers Judging, then the person extraverts the judgment process, and others are likely first to see a drive for decision making through either Thinking or Feeling.
- If a person prefers Perceiving, then the person extraverts the perception process, and others are likely first to see a desire for information gathering through either Sensing or Intuition.

Knowing which function in the type is Extraverted helps to identify the order of the functions. We have already seen that

- a person who prefers Extraversion uses the dominant function in an Extraverted way, and the auxiliary function in an Introverted way
- a person who prefers Introversion uses the dominant function in an Introverted way, and the auxiliary function in an Extraverted way

If we know that Judging or Perceiving identifies the Extraverted function, then we also know that the Judging or Perceiving preference identifies

- the dominant function for people who prefer Extraversion
- the auxiliary function for people who prefer Introversion

Example of Type Dynamics

This chapter began with an example of whole type for Josie, who has preferences for ESFP. If we apply the principles of type dynamics, we see the interactions of preferences for an ESFP.

An ESFP type code shows *balance* between the processes of perception and judgment. The two middle letters are S (Sensing) and F (Feeling). Sensing is a perception process used for information gathering. Feeling is a judgment process used for decision making.

Type dynamics principles state that one of the two middle preferences of the type code is used in an Extraverted way and the other in an Introverted way. To identify which function is used in the Extraverted way, we look at the last letter of the type code, in this case P (Perceiving). The Perceiving preference indicates that the perception process is the Extraverted process. For an ESFP the perception process is Sensing. The Extraverted function for ESFP is Sensing, and the type achieves balance by using the Feeling function in an Introverted way.

To identify the *hierarchy of the functions*, we look at the first letter of the type code, in this case E. A person who prefers Extraversion uses the lead (dominant) function in an extraverted way. For an ESFP the Extraverted function is Sensing, which is the dominant function. A person who prefers Extraversion uses the second (auxiliary) function in an Introverted way. For an ESFP the Introverted function is Feeling, which is the auxiliary function. (Note that the Extraverted function is the dominant function only for Extraverts. For Introverts, the Extraverted function is the auxiliary function, and the Introverted function is the dominant function.)

The third and fourth functions are not named in the type code but are part of the type dynamics hierarchy. The third (tertiary function) is on the same dichotomy as the auxiliary function. For an ESFP the auxiliary function is Introverted Feeling, and the third function is Thinking. The fourth function is on the same dichotomy as the dominant function, but in the opposite attitude. For an ESFP, the dominant function is Extraverted Sensing, and the fourth function is Introverted Intuition.

Putting together all four functions, then, the hierarchy of the functions for ESFP looks like this:

Dominant function	Extraverted Sensing	S_E
Auxiliary function	Introverted Feeling	F_I
Third function	Thinking	T
Fourth function	Introverted Intuition	N_I

Note that the Extraverted or Introverted expression of each function is shown by a subscript E or I after the letter symbol of the function. For example, Extraverted Sensing is shown as S_E and Introverted Feeling, as F_I. Abbreviations for the preferences and attitudes will be used throughout the remainder of this book when showing the type dynamics or communication information.

Order of Functions for Each Type

Myers and Briggs developed a formula to identify the order of the functions as one considers type dynamics. Table 7.2 (page 102) shows this order for each of the sixteen types.

While a table of the order of functions names only the four preferences of Sensing, Intuition, Thinking, and Feeling, the formula to identify the order takes into account contributions of Extraversion or Introversion and of Judging

table 7.2
Order and Direction of Functions in Each Type

	ISTJ		ISFJ		INFJ		INTJ	
Dominant	Sensing	I	Sensing	I	Intuition	I	Intuition	I
Auxiliary	Thinking	E	Feeling	E	Feeling	E	Thinking	E
Third	Feeling		Thinking		Thinking		Feeling	
Fourth	Intuition	E	Intuition	E	Sensing	E	Sensing	E
Dominant	**ISTP** Thinking	I	**ISFP** Feeling	I	**INFP** Feeling	I	**INTP** Thinking	I
Auxiliary	Sensing	E	Sensing	E	Intuition	E	Intuition	E
Third	Intuition		Intuition		Sensing		Sensing	
Fourth	Feeling	E	Thinking	E	Thinking	E	Feeling	E
Dominant	**ESTP** Sensing	E	**ESFP** Sensing	E	**ENFP** Intuition	E	**ENTP** Intuition	E
Auxiliary	Thinking	I	Feeling	I	Feeling	I	Thinking	I
Third	Feeling		Thinking		Thinking		Feeling	
Fourth	Intuition	I	Intuition	I	Sensing	I	Sensing	I
Dominant	**ESTJ** Thinking	E	**ESFJ** Feeling	E	**ENFJ** Feeling	E	**ENTJ** Thinking	E
Auxiliary	Sensing	I	Sensing	I	Intuition	I	Intuition	I
Third	Intuition		Intuition		Sensing		Sensing	
Fourth	Feeling	I	Thinking	I	Thinking	I	Feeling	I

or Perceiving in determining the lead and supporting functions.

It includes the concept of balance: having access to one perception function and one judgment function as well as having a balance between Extraversion and Introversion. Balance, as stated earlier, does not mean equality of the functions. In the formula to identify the order of functions, one function takes the lead and the other, a supporting role.

Sometimes the formula to identify the order of functions seems arbitrary, and in a way, it is. However, Myers and Briggs based the formula on careful study of Jung's theory and years of observation of people. Additional observation by many users of type, as well as research studies, continue to provide support for the order of functions shown in the table.

the art of dialogue

chapter 8 implications of type dynamics for communication

Oral communication is an Extraverted activity involving interaction between people. When we understand type dynamics, we recognize that

- people who prefer Extraversion communicate first with their Extraverted dominant function;
- people who prefer Introversion communicate first with their Extraverted auxiliary function.

Another way to say this is that

- Extraverts communicate from their best-developed function;
- Introverts communicate from their second-best developed function.

A Theory about Type and Communication

Early in the study of type and communication, researchers and type users recognized that not all preferences have an equal role in communication. Flavil R. Yeakley, Jr., (1982, 1983, 1998) developed a theory about type and communication that has been adopted or adapted by others who are also interested in the study of type and communication. Yeakley's theory proposes the following:

- Communication essentially involves the four functions—Sensing, Intuition, Thinking, and Feeling.
- The primary communication function is the Extraverted function for each type.

- Extraverted *dominant* function for Extraverts.
- Extraverted *auxiliary* function for Introverts.
- The secondary communication function is the Introverted function.
  - Introverted *auxiliary* function for Extraverts.
  - Introverted *dominant* function for Introverts.
- The third communication function is the third function.
- The least-preferred communication function is the least-preferred or fourth function.
- A person can and does use any function in communication, but increasing effort is required as the person moves through the order of the communication functions.
- The farther that the sender of communication must move from his or her own primary communication function to reach the primary function of the receiver, the more difficult the communication is.
- Ease of communication between two people is not always the same in both directions; that is, even between the same two people, communication adaptations can be harder for one person than for the other.

Based on Yeakley's theory, it is possible to assess the relative ease or difficulty of communication between any two types. Yeakley offers a quick method to evaluate communication between two people.

- If the two middle letters of the MBTI® types are the same, communication is likely to be relatively easy.
- If one middle letter is the same but the other middle letter is different, communication is likely to be moderately difficult.
- If the two middle letters are both different, communication is likely to be much more difficult.

A more precise way of assessing relative ease or difficulty of communication takes into account the hierarchical order of the communication functions for each type. This information is shown in tables 8.1 and 8.2, which identify the type dynamics and the communication functions for each type. Using this additional information, we see that, for Extraverts, the type dynamics and the communication functions are in the same order. For Introverts, however, the order differs.

Power of the Extraverted Dominant Function
The Extraverted activity of oral communication draws on the strengths of

table 8.1
Order and Direction of Functions in Each Type

	ISTJ	ISFJ	INFJ	INTJ
Dominant	Sensing I	Sensing I	Intuition I	Intuition I
Auxiliary	Thinking E	Feeling E	Feeling E	Thinking E
Third	Feeling	Thinking	Thinking	Feeling
Fourth	Intuition E	Intuition E	Sensing E	Sensing E

	ISTP	ISFP	INFP	INTP
Dominant	Thinking I	Feeling I	Feeling I	Thinking I
Auxiliary	Sensing E	Sensing E	Intuition E	Intuition E
Third	Intuition	Intuition	Sensing	Sensing
Fourth	Feeling E	Thinking E	Thinking E	Feeling E

	ESTP	ESFP	ENFP	ENTP
Dominant	Sensing E	Sensing E	Intuition E	Intuition E
Auxiliary	Thinking I	Feeling I	Feeling I	Thinking I
Third	Feeling	Thinking	Thinking	Feeling
Fourth	Intuition I	Intuition I	Sensing I	Sensing I

	ESTJ	ESFJ	ENFJ	ENTJ
Dominant	Thinking E	Feeling E	Feeling E	Thinking E
Auxiliary	Sensing I	Sensing I	Intuition I	Intuition I
Third	Intuition	Intuition	Sensing	Sensing
Fourth	Feeling I	Thinking I	Thinking I	Feeling I

table 8.2
Order and Direction of Communication Functions in Each Type

	ISTJ	ISFJ	INFJ	INTJ
Primary	Thinking E	Feeling E	Feeling E	Thinking E
Secondary	Sensing I	Sensing I	Intuition I	Intuition I
Third	Feeling	Thinking	Thinking	Feeling
Fourth	Intuition E	Intuition E	Sensing E	Sensing E

	ISTP	ISFP	INFP	INTP
Primary	Sensing E	Sensing E	Intuition E	Intuition E
Secondary	Thinking I	Feeling I	Feeling I	Thinking I
Third	Intuition	Intuition	Sensing	Sensing
Fourth	Feeling E	Thinking E	Thinking E	Feeling E

	ESTP	ESFP	ENFP	ENTP
Primary	Sensing E	Sensing E	Intuition E	Intuition E
Secondary	Thinking I	Feeling I	Feeling I	Thinking I
Third	Feeling	Thinking	Thinking	Feeling
Fourth	Intuition I	Intuition I	Sensing I	Sensing I

	ESTJ	ESFJ	ENFJ	ENTJ
Primary	Thinking E	Feeling E	Feeling E	Thinking E
Secondary	Sensing I	Sensing I	Intuition I	Intuition I
Third	Intuition	Intuition	Sensing	Sensing
Fourth	Feeling I	Thinking I	Thinking I	Feeling I

people who have a preference for Extraversion. From the perspective of type dynamics, their dominant function is Extraverted. From the perspective of communication, their primary Extraverted function is their dominant function. When the dominant function and the primary communication function are the same, we have a powerful combination and tend to see ready clues to the function's identity.

Dominant Extraverted Thinking. Sherad (ESTJ) noticed that a chair had been moved from his home office to another room. His first reaction was to ask, "What were the benefits of moving the desk chair?"

Following are the type dynamics for ESTJ:

Dominant function	T_E
Auxiliary function	S_I
Third function	N
Fourth function	F_I

For Sherad Thinking is both the Extraverted function and the dominant function. His first comment was from dominant Extraverted Thinking. He wanted to know the reasons—both pros and cons—for moving the chair, explicitly asking about the benefits and implicitly about the disadvantages.

Dominant Extraverted Feeling. Enola (ENFJ) was going through a tense time with a friend. When Enola approached a mutual friend, her first words were, "Can you help me understand what is going on?"

The type dynamics for ENFJ look like this:

Dominant function	F_E
Auxiliary function	N_I
Third function	S
Fourth function	T_I

For Enola, Feeling is both the Extraverted function and the dominant function. Her first words were from dominant Extraverted Feeling—asking for help to restore harmony to a strained interpersonal relationship.

Extraverted Dominant Functions in Conflict

Extraverted dominant functions not only provide readily heard clues to their identity but also reveal sources of conflict. The following example of the married couple Irma and Maynard illustrates the power of the dominant function and what can happen when dominant functions are in conflict.

106

Irma has preferences for ESFJ and Maynard for ESTJ. The type dynamics for each of them look like this:

	Irma, ESFJ	Maynard, ESTJ
Dominant function	F_E	T_E
Auxiliary function	S_I	S_I
Third function	N	N
Fourth function	T_I	F_I

A first glance at Irma's and Maynard's type preferences suggests that communication should be relatively easy. They have three preferences in common—E, S, and J. They tend to see the world in the same way through their Sensing preference, with a focus on realistic, practical facts. However, Irma's and Maynard's dominant functions differ.

One way Irma expresses her dominant Feeling function is through her joy in setting a pretty table for dinner guests. She especially enjoys serving a dessert with a vanilla sauce that she puts in a small pitcher that belonged to her grandmother.

At a recent dinner party, Irma brought the sauce pitcher to the table. As she set dessert bowls before the guests, Maynard picked up the pitcher, went to the kitchen, and returned with the sauce in a measuring cup. The following dialogue took place.

Irma: Maynard!

Maynard: The pitcher always drips. This is easier to pour and won't get drips on the linen tablecloth.

Irma: But it's a measuring cup! Why do you hurt me so? We have guests.

Maynard: (later after guests are gone) Why do you have to make an emotional scene in front of guests?

 **LISTENING FOR TYPE CLUES.** For Irma, who has a dominant Feeling function, what is most important is remembering her relationship with her grandmother and setting a pretty table for guests. Irma is hurt that Maynard does not share her values.

For Maynard, who has a dominant Thinking function, what is most important is being logical. He considers a pitcher that drips to be illogical. His logical solution is to pour the sauce into a cup that does not drip. Maynard is upset that Irma rejects his logic and expresses her hurt in front of guests.

APPLYING TYPE: *Type differences are real.* It is important to remember that having a preference for Feeling does not mean being emotional. Feeling has to do with making rational decisions based on person-centered values. Irma made a decision to use the pitcher based on values that were important to her. Her emotions are an expression of frustration that Maynard does not share, understand, or accept the values on which she based her decision.

Irma and Maynard have only a limited knowledge of type. It is possible that a deeper understanding could help them communicate more effectively about their differences.

It is important to remember, however, that an understanding of type would not eliminate differences. Type differences are real. Lloyd Edwards (1993) notes that if we accept type differences between people as real, legitimate, and significant, then

- conflict is inevitable; conflict does not mean hostility, but it does include the interplay of differences;
- differences do not go away with education, persuasion, or coercion;
- there is a need to understand differences and how to live with them.

Incidents such as the one between Irma and Maynard are likely to recur in a long-term relationship. Nevertheless, type understanding can be a starting point for communication about differences. In this case, the motivational driving force of the dominant function is also the primary Extraverted communication function for each of them. For Irma and Maynard, understanding sources of frustration and conflict begins with recognition of the real differences in the cores of their psychological types.

When we see type differences such as those that exist between Maynard and Irma, we may be tempted to assume that type can identify which combinations of personality types are more successful or less successful in relationships. Observations and studies both indicate that any possible combination of types can and do have successful relationships. Paul Tieger and Barbara Barron-Tieger (2000) interviewed couples of all possible type combinations. They found satisfaction among couples in both short-term and long-term relationships among all combinations of personality types.

Usually, the more type preferences a couple has in common, the more likely it is that each partner sees and acts in the world in similar ways. The more type preferences that are different, the more resources the couple is likely to have. In other words, when type preferences are different, the blind spot of one is likely to be a strength of the other, so that together the couple has a way to move through situations rather than both being stuck in the same way. Maynard and Irma find strength in their relationship through common interests, skills, and values derived from the auxiliary Introverted Sensing function, which they share. Despite clashes of their different Extraverted dominant functions (Thinking for Maynard and Feeling for Irma), they have had a loving marriage of more than sixty years.

In general, it is best to consider that love is type blind. After a couple falls in love, type can help bring understanding to the similarities and differences, and type dynamics can enhance the depth of understanding.

Type Dynamics and Communication in Introverts

The primary communication function and the dominant function are the same for Extraverts. However, communication and type dynamics are more complex for Introverts. The following personal example illustrates Yeakley's communication theory using type dynamics for Introverts.

My type preferences are for INFP. Ray, my husband, has preferences for ISFJ. Because we both have a preference for Introversion, the order between our type dynamics and communication functions differs. The type dynamics and communication functions for our types look like this:

Carolyn, INFP				Ray, ISFJ			
Type Dynamics		Communication		Type Dynamics		Communication	
Dominant	F_I	Primary	N	Dominant	S_I	Primary	F
Auxiliary	N_E	Secondary	F	Auxiliary	F_E	Secondary	S
Third	S	Third	S	Third	T	Third	T
Fourth	T_E	Fourth	T	Fourth	N_E	Fourth	N

If we use Yeakley's quick method to evaluate communication, we see that one middle letter in our MBTI types is the same. Ray and I both have a preference for Feeling. According to Yeakley's theory, communication is likely to be moderately difficult for us.

Ray and I have different preferences on the Sensing-Intuition dichotomy, so that we view the world from different perspectives. I see the world in a broad brushstroke way that looks for patterns and summarizing ideas. Ray sees the world in terms of specifics and details. These differences tend to be both evident and transparent in our conversations. We often readily recognize the differences and use them as resources. Together we can explore an idea from more than one perspective. Our common Feeling preference is helpful when we make decisions based on person-centered values, seek consensus, and focus on harmony and relationships.

When we go to the next steps of Yeakley's theory and consider the order of communication functions, we see that communication is more complex for us. Ray and I both prefer Introversion. For the Extraverted interaction of communication, we go first to our Extraverted auxiliary functions—Intuition for me, Feeling for Ray. Even after years of marriage and of studying and applying psychological type, we hear ourselves using these functions, particularly when we introduce new topics of conversation.

At this point we also experience another aspect of the communication theory. Yeakley says that ease of communication between two people is not always the same in both directions. When we trace the communication patterns for Ray and me, as shown in figures 8.1 and 8.2, we can begin to understand Yeakley's statement.

figure 8.1
Stretch of Communication Functions: Carolyn to Ray

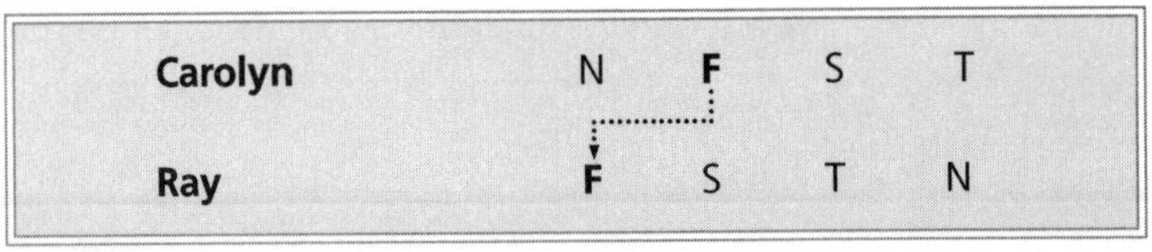

Carolyn	N	**F**	S	T
Ray	**F**	S	T	N

figure 8.2
Stretch of Communication Functions: Ray to Carolyn

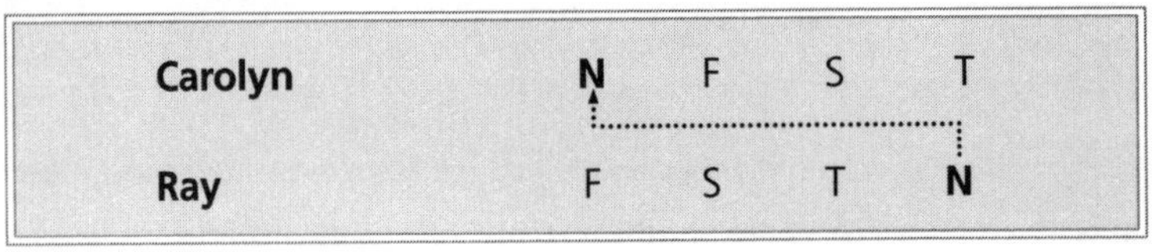

Carolyn	**N**	F	S	T
Ray	F	S	T	**N**

If I really want to get across a message to Ray and need to adapt to Ray's primary communication function, I can make a relatively small adjustment (figure 8.1). I need to move only to my secondary communication function.

If Ray really wants to get across a message to me and needs to adapt to my primary communication function, he must make a much greater adjustment

the art of dialogue

than I must make (figure 8.2). To speak to me, he must stretch all the way to his fourth function—the function that is least developed and least comfortable. Years of experience confirm for us that it is more difficult for Ray to communicate with me than for me to communicate with him.

One way to deal with Ray's greater difficulty in communication is for us to agree to return to our common Feeling preference. From a communication perspective, this allows Ray to use his primary communication function and allows me to use my secondary communication function—a short stretch for me. At first glance, this also seems to make sense from a type dynamics perspective. Ray can speak from his Extraverted auxiliary function, and I can use my dominant function, which has a natural motivation to seek Feeling content.

Looking further at type dynamics, we see that Ray and I both prefer Introversion. Oral communication is an Extraverted activity and so is more complicated for Introverts than for Extraverts. When Ray speaks from Extraverted Feeling, he uses his primary communication function, but this is his auxiliary function in terms of type dynamics. He converses about his second most important content and processes his most important content inside himself. When I communicate with the Feeling function, I use my dominant function of Introverted Feeling, but this is my secondary communication function. I try to say aloud the content that I more naturally process in the secure comfort of my inner world.

In a long-term relationship such as ours, Ray and I periodically do need a purposeful check-in to say what is really going on inside us and sometimes do converse from our Introverted dominant functions. Still, much of our conversation flows from our Extraverted auxiliary functions, which are our primary communication channels.

The interaction of communication and type dynamics theories helps us understand and resolve many communication issues. Understanding the effect of type preferences smoothes the way for much of our communication. We have resources of different perspectives in our Sensing and Intuition functions, as well as common ground in our shared Feeling function. Understanding our differences in ease or difficulty of communication can help us recognize possible sources of frustration even as we attempt to adapt to the communication approach of the other. Understanding that as Introverts we communicate primarily from our auxiliary functions helps us recognize the need to occasionally check in with our Introverted dominant functions. While communication is a complex process, understanding communication and type dynamics theories can enhance the communication process.

Research Studies

This chapter began with a summary of a theory developed by Yeakley about type and communication. The chapter ends with a summary of some of the research that tested the hypotheses of the theory that communication functions affect effective communication.

Early in his work with type and communication, Yeakley conducted a series of six studies in different settings, each of which supported his theory. These studies involved communication in

- marriages, with ninety couples in counseling situations;
- organizations, with thirty managers and thirty subordinates;
- discussion classes, with twelve teachers and 266 students;
- lecture classes, with twelve teachers and 661 students;
- sales situations, with ten life insurance sales representatives, twenty prospects who had recently purchased insurance, and twenty prospects who had heard a sales presentation but had not purchased insurance; and
- religious settings, with sixteen clergy and fifty recent new adult members in each minister's congregation.

Each study supported Yeakley's type and communication theory.

- Couples who were judged by marriage counselors to have the greatest improvement in their relationships after six months of counseling had more similarities in communication functions than couples with little or no improvement.
- Managers and subordinates who rated their communication as successful had more similarities in communication functions than those who rated their communication as mixed or unsuccessful.
- In both discussion and lecture classes, a student's grade in the course was higher than was likely to be expected relative to the student's previous grade-point average when there was greater similarity in communication function between teacher and student.
- Sales representatives had more similarities in communication functions with prospects who purchased insurance than with prospects who heard the sales presentation but did not purchase insurance.
- New members of church congregations had more similarities in communication function with the minister, whatever the minister's type.

The study of religious communication offers an example of the complexity of communication research. To minimize biasing factors, clergy persons were all from the same denomination in the Christian religion, were all in cities that had more than one church of that denomination, were all in relatively large congregations (500–2000 members), and had all been in their current churches five to nine years. Having set these parameters, the researcher selected one clergy person of each of the sixteen types—no small task since some types have very low representation among clergy. From each church, the researcher drew a random sample of fifty new adult members who had affiliated with the congregation during the tenure of the clergy person. The researcher developed a numerical scoring system based on the theoretical ease or difficulty of communication between any two types. This system was used in all six original studies. In the religious communication study, there was a relatively close match between the communication function of each clergy person and a majority of the fifty people in the random sample of new adult members in that clergy person's church. Careful research studies such as this one contribute evidence in support of Yeakley's theory about psychological type and communication.

A Note about Yeakley's Work

Some readers who are familiar with Yeakley's work are aware than an early replication study found some differences in results. Analysis of the research showed a need for minor adjustments in the formula used to score ease or difficulty of communication. Later research using the adjusted scoring system supported the original theory.

chapter 9 extraverted and introverted expressions of functions

Type dynamics is a structural model that explains how the preferences of psychological type interact with each other in a dynamic whole. The theories of type dynamics and communication state that not all preferences have equal weight, that the functions represent the core of type, that the functions have a hierarchical order, and that a type includes balance. The theories explain differences in communication for Extraverts and Introverts.

Type dynamics and communication theories also help us understand differences in the Extraverted and Introverted expressions of functions. In this chapter we explore differences in people who prefer the same function but in different attitudes. Type dynamics helps us see how people who Extravert a particular function are likely to express the general characteristics differently than those who Introvert the same function. For example, patterns of differences exist between Extraverted Sensing and Introverted Sensing. Table 9.1 (page 116) lists some of the differences between the Extraverted and Introverted expressions of each of the four functions.

Extraverted and Introverted Functions in Action

The stories that follow illustrate differences between Extraverted and Introverted expressions of the Sensing, Intuition, Thinking, and Feeling functions.

table 9.1

Extraverted and Introverted Expressions of Functions

People Who Prefer Extraverted Sensing (S_E) tend to	People Who Prefer Introverted Sensing (S_I) tend to
• focus on the present moment, the here and now	• relate current events to past experiences
• be observant of the external physical environment	• have large private fact collections
• accurately notice details that can be observed with the five senses	• be patient with details and find satisfaction in accurately organizing data
• be willing to do whatever is useful to get the greatest result with the least effort	• prefer tangible, concrete facts, verified by experience, and may be cautious about going beyond facts
• focus on pragmatic actions and techniques based on experience	• trust legitimate authority and standard operating procedures
• value adventure, variety, and skillful performance	• value responsibility and dependability
• learn best through practical, hands-on experience	• learn best by gathering all the pieces of information and seeing how they fit together
• value aesthetics and find enjoyment in material things	• value traditions and stability
People Who Prefer Extraverted Intuition (N_E) tend to	People Who Prefer Introverted Intuition (N_I) tend to
• generate possibilities	• see patterns, relationships, and connections
• look for the big picture and global concepts	• see underlying meanings and read between the lines
• find that sense impressions of the moment trigger flights of the imagination	• be fully aware only of sense impressions related to the inspiration of the moment
• energize others; be seen as resourceful	• provide long-range vision and depth of understanding; be seen as insightful
• be energized by brainstorming	• be energized by solving new problems
People Who Prefer Extraverted Thinking (T_E) tend to	People Who Prefer Introverted Thinking (T_I) tend to
• organize information and the environment into a logical structure	• evaluate information with analysis according to principles, criteria, and objective standards
• create and critique systems, procedures, and models	• categorize information and see inconsistencies
• express interest by challenging facts and ideas, offering opinions directly, and debating pros and cons	• express thoughts when asked or when logic or decisions are challenged
• expect competency and efficiency	• be highly self-critical

the art of dialogue

People Who Prefer Extraverted Feeling (F$_E$) tend to	People Who Prefer Introverted Feeling (F$_I$) tend to
• seek harmony first in relationships with others and then with their own values	• seek harmony first in their values and then in relationships with others
• have a need for cooperation and supportive interaction with others	• have a need for authenticity, meaning and significance in their lives
• organize structures and environments to meet the needs of others	• support the needs of others quietly and through example
• seek inclusiveness through warmth, empathy, and interest	• trust and be committed to others who share their convictions

The type clues sections following each story include a discussion of the order of functions for each type represented in the story as well as identification of characteristics of the Extraverted and Introverted functions that are revealed in the communication.

Extraverted Sensing (S$_E$) and Introverted Sensing (S$_I$): What Did You See?

In the following story we hear a conversation between two people who both have a Sensing preference. Bonita (ESFP) uses Sensing in an Extraverted way, focusing on people and activities around her. Martin (ISFJ) uses Sensing in an Introverted way, focusing on thoughts and memories.

Bonita and Martin were eating breakfast. Bonita observed Martin open the refrigerator, look at the butter shelf in the door, take something from the back of the bottom shelf of the refrigerator, close the door, and come to the table with an unopened tub of margarine.

Bonita: Are you planning to eat so much margarine that you need two tubs open?

Martin: This is just one tub.

Bonita: But why are you getting another new one?

Martin: I finished the old one yesterday.

Bonita: I know, but I opened a new one and put it on the butter shelf last night.

Martin: I didn't see it.

Bonita: How could you not see it? I saw you look right at it.

Martin: I didn't see it.

LISTENING FOR TYPE CLUES. Both Bonita and Martin have Sensing as their dominant functions, but Bonita extraverts the Sensing preference, and Martin introverts the Sensing preference. The type dynamics for Bonita and Martin look like this:

	Bonita, ESFP	Martin, ISFJ
Dominant function	S_E	S_I
Auxiliary function	F_I	F_E
Third function	T	T
Fourth function	N_I	N_E

Bonita extraverts her dominant function and first focuses her attention on observing what goes on around her. She makes observations about the physical details of Martin's actions—looking at the butter shelf and reaching to the back of the bottom shelf for a margarine tub.

Martin introverts Sensing and first focuses his attention inward to his memories and thoughts. When Martin reports that he did not see a tub of margarine on the butter shelf although Bonita saw him looking at it, Martin is telling the truth. When he opened the refrigerator door to reach for margarine, he remembered that yesterday he had finished the old tub and would need to start a new one today. The memory was so clear that he indeed did not see the new margarine tub that Bonita had set on the shelf.

Extraverted Sensing (S_E): Paying Attention to What Is Around You

In the following story, five people all speak from Extraverted Sensing. For two of the people, Extraverted Sensing is the dominant function. For one of them it is the auxiliary function, and for two of them, Sensing is the third function. As we listen to the conversation, we need to remember that each person has access to and can use all of the functions. We hear each person speak about details that the individual perceives from the environment through the five senses.

Jason (ESFP), Travis (ESTP), Dustin (ISTP), Kirk (INFP), and Max (ENFJ) are shooting the breeze at a company picnic.

Max: Hey, Dustin, you took that new training course, didn't you? How was it?

Dustin: It had some useful information, but what irritated me was all the noise the examiner made during the test. He'd just said the room was to be quiet, and then he kept shuffling papers, pouring glasses of water, and pacing around the room. It was bad enough that the chairs were hard and the air conditioning blew out a blast of cold air every time it kicked on, but the examiner's distracting noises really ticked me off.

Kirk: I've taken tests from him before, but I just tune him out.

Dustin: Nothing personal, but I really get irritated when someone tells me to just ignore the distractions.

Jason: Yeah, usually little stuff irritates most. My wife and I argue whenever I buy a new shirt.

Travis: Hey, man! She doesn't like the prices of those silk shirts and plush pullovers you wear.

Jason: She doesn't talk about prices. She says it's ridiculous that the first thing I do is cut out all the tags. It irritates me when I buy clothes that feel good, and then they have scratchy tags. She also says I waste water because I wash new clothes before I wear them. I don't like that new stiffness.

Travis: My wife is happy that I do most of the laundry, especially the ironing. She knows I'm particular about the crease in our uniforms. But she says I waste water on me. I like a good long shower. It washes away all the gunk from work. Pun intended. My folks used to make me be last. They said if I was first, no one else got a hot shower.

Jason: My way to get away from work is to climb on my motorcycle and feel the wind in my face and blowing through my hair.

Travis: How long have you had that machine?

Jason: My current one? A year next week, but I've been riding cycles ever since I was big enough to get on.

Kirk: That seems more dangerous than I'm comfortable with. I like walking in wooded areas. I've always liked the peace and quiet, but in

extraverted and introverted expressions of functions

recent years autumn is my favorite time—crunching through the leaves under a blue autumn sky. The sky isn't quite that color of blue any other time of year. Sometimes I rake up piles of leaves in the yard just so the kids and I can jump in them.

Max: My best relaxation the last few years is when I work in my garden. I like the feel and smell of the earth. My favorite spot is my herb garden. I like to rub the leaves, feel the textures, smell the scents.

Jason: I like cooking with herbs. A good blend really brings out the flavor of food.

Travis: Speaking of food, I'm going to get some. Good food, good friends, you know.

LISTENING FOR TYPE CLUES. All the irritants, skills, and favorite activities the men mention in this conversation are expressions of Extraverted Sensing. Jason, Travis, and Dustin all report Extraverted Sensing in their MBTI® types. The type dynamics look like this:

	Jason, ESFP	Travis, ESTP	Dustin, ISTP
Dominant function	S_E	S_E	T_I
Auxiliary function	F_I	T_I	S_E
Third function	T	F	N
Fourth function	N_I	N_I	F_E

Jason and Travis both have Extraverted Sensing as their dominant functions. The feel of scratchy tags and stiff fabric on Jason's skin irritates him. He enjoys the feel of the wind on his face and in his hair, while Travis enjoys perfect creases in his uniforms and the feel of water on his skin. Both savor the taste of good food. Both indicate that they have been tuned into Sensing experiences most of their lives.

For Dustin, Extraverted Sensing is the auxiliary function. A common misconception is that an Introvert lives inside his own head to such an extent that he tunes out what is going on around him. Dustin's preferred mode in the exam setting is to use his Thinking function inside his head, but in the quiet of the examination room, his Extraverted Sensing function is alert to all the distractions he perceives with his senses—shuffling papers, water being poured into a glass, footsteps, hard chairs, and cold air.

Neither Kirk (INFP) nor Max (ENFJ) have Sensing preferences in their type codes, but in this conversation, both speak from Extraverted Sensing. Kirk enjoys the crunch of crisp leaves and the specific shade of blue of the autumn sky. Max enjoys the feel and smell of the earth and herbs.

 APPLYING TYPE: *Development of the third function.* Both Kirk and Max indicate that experiencing Sensing is relatively recent for them. We can hypothesize that both are at a place in their lives where they are developing the third function. The type dynamics for Kirk and Max look like this:

	Kirk, INFP	Max, ENFJ
Dominant function	F_I	F_E
Auxiliary function	N_E	N_I
Third function	S	S
Fourth function	T_E	T_I

Kirk and Max have found nonessential ways to experiment with this relatively immature function. Their livelihood does not appear to depend on skill with the third function. Instead, they find ways to enjoy playful, recreational experiences that allow them to develop it.

Extraverted Intuition (N_E) and Introverted Intuition (N_I): How Do the Ideas Connect?

Ali (INFJ) described her experience listening to a speaker at a conference. As we hear her tell what she heard from the speaker and what she expected but did not hear, we find clues to differences in attitude of the Intuition function between Ali and the speaker.

> **Ali:** The keynote speaker was good, I think. He had a lot of ideas, but he just gave one after the other. It was, "You could do this," "Some people do that," or "Here's something else that's interesting." At the end of the speech, I wondered what his point was. I couldn't see a connection between one idea and the next. I'm supposed to give a report on the conference at our next staff meeting. I don't know how I can summarize that speech.

LISTENING FOR TYPE CLUES. We can hypothesize that the conference speaker has a preference for Extraverted Intuition. The speaker moves from one possibility to the next. It is likely that he assumes different people in his audience have different interests and that each will find a different idea interesting or useful.

Ali (INFJ) has a preference for Introverted Intuition. The type dynamics look like this:

Dominant function	N_I
Auxiliary function	F_E
Third function	T
Fourth function	S_E

Using her dominant Introverted Intuition, Ali seeks first the relationships between ideas and the patterns among possibilities. With her Extraverted judgment function (Feeling), she has a tendency to conduct an initial evaluation of ideas as she hears them and to begin ordering the possibilities according to patterns she identifies.

APPLYING TYPE: *Same function, different attitudes.* Although Ali and the speaker both have preferences for Intuition, Ali has difficulty understanding his speech. She perceives the speaker's approach as being similar to brainstorming, with ideas popping up as they come to mind, in no particular order. She wants the speaker to show how the possibilities relate to each other and how they support a clearly stated main point.

Differences between different preferences on a dichotomy tend to be apparent. If one person has a preference for Sensing and another person for Intuition, we expect to see differences and are aware of them. Differences that arise from different attitudes on the same function are more difficult to recognize. If two people both have a preference for Intuition, we expect to see—and usually do see—much in common. We may be surprised by the differences we see in the ways the two people express the Intuition preference. It is helpful to remember that no two people are exactly alike—even if they prefer the same function in the same attitude. It is also helpful to recognize differences associated with the Extraverted and Introverted attitudes of the functions.

Extraverted Thinking (T_E) and Introverted Thinking (T_I): What's the Reason?

People who extravert the Thinking function tend to organize information and the environment into a logical structure and to express opinions directly. People who introvert the Thinking function tend to evaluate information with analysis and to express thoughts based on that analysis if their decision or logic is challenged. In the following dialogue, we hear an exchange between Fred (ESTJ), who extraverts Thinking, and Tyler (ESTP), who introverts Thinking.

Fred is commander of an army reserve combat training unit. He calls a first lieutenant in the unit, thirty-five-year-old Tyler, to report to his office.

Fred: Ty, you know there could be a reserve call-up. The battalion needs a team to prepare for the call-up if it comes. I'm asking you to be on that team.

Tyler: You're activating me? Or you're asking me to volunteer to go active? Which is it?

Fred: For now, volunteer.

Tyler: Starting when? For how long?

Fred: A year. Current activation date is next Tuesday, but that could change.

Tyler: Where? Any extra pay in this? Any promotions? What's the assignment?

Tyler: (after hearing Fred's answers) Hey, man, I'll go if that's orders, but I can't volunteer now.

Fred: Ty, they're handpicking the best for this team. The brigade sergeant major and brigade commander and battalion commander all named you.

Tyler: What's up with the butter-up job?

Fred: You're the right person. I thought I could count on you. You've always been a go-with-the-action man.

Tyler: I'm almost done with work to transfer to civil affairs. This assignment would take me off track and postpone that. I'm getting older. I'm not necessarily interested in being 100 percent combat oriented any more.

Fred: You're the best first lieutenant in the division. You want to leave that for civil affairs?

Tyler: It's just the whole aspect of being able to work with people. So often the media doesn't show what the military does to help others. It's not logical, but that's the way it is. I figure in civil affairs maybe I can do something that helps people and dispels some myths.

LISTENING FOR TYPE CLUES. Fred and Tyler both have preferences for Thinking. For Fred, Thinking is Extraverted and is the dominant function. For Tyler, Thinking is Introverted and is the auxiliary function. The type dynamics look like this:

	Fred, ESTJ	Tyler, ESTP
Dominant function	T_E	S_E
Auxiliary function	S_I	T_I
Third function	N	F
Fourth function	F_I	N_I

Fred, whose dominant function and primary communication function is Extraverted Thinking, focuses first on the purpose, task, and structure of the battalion. He begins the conversation with a reasoned decision—that Tyler is needed as a volunteer to implement the task and structure. When Tyler declines, Fred states additional reasons for the request—that Tyler has been handpicked, that he is a go-with-the-action man, and that he is the best first lieutenant in the division.

Tyler begins the conversation from Extraverted Sensing, which is his dominant function and primary communication function. He asks for specific information—when? how long? where? what? He then uses his Introverted Thinking function to evaluate Fred's answers. He is skeptical about Fred's attempt to butter him up. He weighs the consequences of accepting the volunteer assignment—that it would delay reaching his goal. When Fred challenges Tyler's decision, Tyler states his reasons for sticking to his goal of working in civil affairs.

APPLYING TYPE: *Type development.* Listening to Tyler's reasons for moving to civil affairs provides clues not only about type preferences but also about type development. Tyler wants to work with people and to help others. Type observers will notice that such language is associated with the Feeling function. For Tyler, Feeling is the third function.

Different type theorists have different timetables for a typical type development pattern for the third function, but most experts suggest that develop-

the art of dialogue

ment typically occurs sometime between a person's mid-twenties and early midlife. Isabel Myers believed that a timetable is not important. What is important is that development occurs.

Tyler, thirty-five years old, has made a decision to move into civil affairs—a move which likely is related to development of Feeling, his third function. He is close to reaching his goal, so it appears he has been in the process of developing the third function for a while.

Sometimes when a third function begins to develop, a person finds it compelling enough to make a complete career change so as to be able to predominantly use that function. While it is possible and good to develop skills associated with the third function, it is important to remember that a person's strengths typically come through the dominant and auxiliary functions. For most people, it is helpful to express the third function through activities related to avocation, recreation, volunteer work, or spiritual development.

Though Tyler wants to express his third function, he does not make a complete career change to do it. He stays in the military. He moves to a different role in a familiar setting, where he can continue to use his dominant Sensing and auxiliary Thinking functions while finding some expression for his third Feeling function.

Extraverted Feeling (F_E) and Introverted Feeling (F_I): Harmony

Hunter (INFJ) and Loni (ISFP) attend a family reunion. Phil and his girlfriend, Gabrielle, are also there. Hunter and Loni both have a preference for Feeling, but one extraverts the function and emphasizes harmony in relationships, while the other introverts Feeling and emphasizes harmony with inner values.

> Hunter: (to Loni) Aunt Freda wrote that she was bringing sour cream raisin pie made from Mom's recipe. She remembered I told her once that it was my favorite, but I haven't eaten pie like Mom's in the ten years since she died.
>
> Phil: (coming to the serving table) Hey, this is my lucky day. There's sour cream raisin pie. I'm going to score points with Gabrielle now. She orders it every time we're in a restaurant that has it.
>
> Hunter: You'd better move fast. This is the last piece.
>
> Phil: Thanks, Buddy.
>
> Loni: (to Hunter, after Phil leaves the table) Why did you let him take your pie?

Hunter: It wasn't mine.

Loni: You were ahead of Phil in line. I don't understand. You just said you'd waited ten years for that pie.

Hunter: He wanted it for Gabrielle.

Loni: As if she'd know the difference between Aunt Freda's pie and any piece in any restaurant!

Hunter: It's a piece of pie. It wasn't worth arguing with Phil about it.

LISTENING FOR TYPE CLUES. Hunter and Loni both report Feeling in their type codes. For Hunter, Feeling is Extraverted and is the auxiliary function. For Loni, Feeling is Introverted and is the dominant function. The type dynamics look like this:

	Hunter, INFJ	Loni, ISFP
Dominant function	N_I	F_I
Auxiliary function	F_E	S_E
Third function	T	N
Fourth function	S_E	T_E

Hunter, who has a preference for Extraverted Feeling, focuses more on harmony in relationships with people than on harmony with his inner value system. He is willing to give up something of personal value to him—in this case, the pie—to facilitate Phil's relationship with Gabrielle and to avoid what Hunter thinks is a potential tension point in his relationship with Phil.

Loni, who has a preference for Introverted Feeling, focuses more on harmony with personal values, while harmony with other people is a lesser concern. She feels Hunter should have stood up for his right to the pie, which had special meaning to him and for which he had waited so long.

APPLYING TYPE: *A source of tension.* Differences in attitudes on the Feeling function can be a source of frustration or tension if two people face a conflict between maintaining harmony with others and maintaining harmony with inner values. In such situations, the person who extraverts the Feeling function compromises harmony with inner values in order to maintain harmony with other people. The person who introverts the Feeling function compromises harmony with other people in order to maintain

the art of dialogue

harmony with values. Despite the fact that both have a Feeling preference, the two people may experience tension in their own relationship because of the differences in what each considers most important. In addition, each may feel an inner tension because each has had to give up one part of the harmony that is a vital aspect of the Feeling function.

In the case of Hunter and Loni, Feeling is the auxiliary function for one and the dominant function for the other. However, in a conflict between the two directions of harmony, the difference in hierarchical order generally is less important than the difference in the extraverted and introverted attitudes of the functions.

Effects of Unheard Functions

Communication includes not only what is spoken and heard, but also what is processed inwardly and unheard. Knowing that we can use functions in both Extraverted and Introverted ways provides us with a tool to recognize and understand some of the unheard parts of communication.

Unheard Introverted Thinking (T$_I$)

In the following story, Lavelle makes a decision with her unheard Introverted Thinking function. When team members hear words and see actions only through Lavelle's Extraverted Intuition function but hear nothing of her Introverted decision, they become frustrated. Communication breaks down between Lavelle and the team members.

> Lavelle (ENTP) is a twenty-nine-year-old director of training in an insurance company. She had been hired by the company eight months earlier to establish a training and development office and to lead the necessary reorganization.
>
> Lavelle was energized by a vision to develop a model of progressive levels of training throughout the company. Before long, she had the first level of training ready to roll out. This level would provide uniform training practices for team members to use within each department. All Lavelle had to do was type in some last pieces of information, format the document, and get it to the team.
>
> Lavelle began development of the second level, intended for inter-departmental training. The goal was to help employees understand how their positions integrated with other departments and with the compa-

ny as a whole. She called a meeting of the training team for an information and brainstorming session.

Prior to the meeting, team members asked if they could also discuss the first-level training plan and give feedback during the meeting. Lavelle said she wanted any feedback the team had.

The meeting began with Lavelle's presentation of her goals for the second-level training. When team members raised their concerns with the first-level plan, Lavelle stated that the purpose of this meeting was to begin second-level planning. Team members persisted, saying they wanted to see the first-level plan now.

Lavelle said she had not yet had time to fill in the details. Team members grumbled that if the first plan was so incomplete, it was premature to begin discussion of still another plan. At their insistence, Lavelle called for a break and went to her office to make copies of the draft of the first-level training plan.

 LISTENING FOR TYPE CLUES. The type dynamics for Lavelle's type, ENTP, look like this:

Dominant function	N_E
Auxiliary function	T_I
Third function	F
Fourth function	S_I

Lavelle has a vision for a model of progressive levels of intra- and interdepartmental training, and she appears to enjoy exploring ideas through brainstorming. Such behavior expresses typical characteristics of Extraverted Intuition, which is her dominant function.

When team members request the opportunity to discuss the first-level plan, she states that she wants feedback—that she is open to more information. Team members likely are accustomed to working with Lavelle through discussion and brainstorming. When she says she wants feedback, the statement fits with their expectations of her communication characteristics.

When they get to the meeting, however, team members are surprised and frustrated that Lavelle wants to talk only about the second level of training and that she has not yet completed the first-level plan. They sense a breakdown of communication. The team members' request, Lavelle's initial response, and her actions in the meeting do not match.

the art of dialogue

An understanding of type dynamics helps us gain some insight into this situation. Lavelle's Extraverted function is Intuition. We hear her enthusiasm for new possibilities. We do not hear the effect of her Introverted Thinking function. Lavelle's auxiliary Introverted Thinking function supports the motivation of the dominant function. She decides that although the details are not complete, the first level is finished because the model is complete. Having that decision made, she focuses her openness to new information on the second level of the project.

APPLYING TYPE: *Appropriate use of type.* As stated in earlier chapters, identification of type preferences does not indicate anything about a person's maturity, development, skill, or excellence in use of the preferences, nor does it provide an excuse for inappropriate use of preferences. When Lavelle decides that the first project is complete, she gives only cursory attention to the auxiliary Thinking function. More appropriate use would include analysis of the draft of the first-level plan—looking for inconsistencies, missing pieces, and illogical steps or leaps in logic. Appropriate use would also include analysis of Lavelle's own strengths and less-developed functions. Any effective plan needs to address the impact on people as well as the details that make the plan practical and useful. These tasks require use of the Feeling and Sensing functions—Lavelle's third and fourth functions. Objective analysis of her own skills or lack of skills with Feeling and Sensing tasks could lead Lavelle to a decision to seek feedback and help from her team members on the incomplete plan.

Appropriate use of the Thinking function could also help Lavelle recognize the need to communicate her Introverted Thinking decision to team members. She says nothing at all about her conclusion that the plan is sufficiently complete, and this lack of communication may be the source of greatest frustration for team members. If Lavelle were to tell them her decision, team members might question the wisdom of the conclusion, but they would have a basis for understanding her behavior in moving to a new project. If Lavelle were to use the Introverted Thinking function appropriately, she could minimize breakdowns in communication and enhance the effectiveness of work between herself and team members.

Unheard Introverted Sensing (S_I) and Introverted Feeling (F_I)

Kelsey (ISTJ) is administrator of an organization. He schedules regular Tuesday morning staff meetings with key personnel. Vanessa (ENFP) manages one of the organization's programs. Listen for both the spoken and the unheard parts of their communication.

Kelsey: Here is the agenda for next week's board of directors' meeting. The agenda will go out Friday. You each see the schedule for your reports.

Vanessa: We have to make some changes. My program is last, but we need to be first. Some of the people who will make our presentation have a prior commitment and need to leave early.

Kelsey: This is the order that makes most sense.

Vanessa: Most of the time it does make sense, but not this time. The board meeting and our meeting with community coordinators usually fall on different days. If we could go first, our people could make both meetings. I understand the importance of the board meeting, but the key to our program's success is regular contact with the community coordinators.

Kelsey: This is the agenda that works. You'll just have to change the other meeting or find a different way to report to the board.

(On Thursday Vanessa received a revised agenda with a note, "See me.")

Kelsey: I've been thinking about your program. It's one of the success stories of this organization, and the board should hear about it from the people who know most about it. It's also true that a key to the success of your program is meeting regularly with community leaders. It seems to me if you report to the board first, then you can also meet with the community leaders. What do you think? Will that work?

 LISTENING FOR TYPE CLUES. Vanessa's type preferences are ENFP and Kelsey's are ISTJ. The type dynamics look like this:

	Vanessa, ENFP	Kelsey, ISTJ
Dominant function	N_E	S_I
Auxiliary function	F_I	T_E
Third function	T	F
Fourth function	S_I	N_E

Vanessa, who extraverts her dominant Intuition function, offers an option as soon as she sees a problem. The two aspects of the problem she identifies arise from her auxiliary Introverted Feeling function. One is the impact of the proposed agenda on the people in her program. A second is the impact on a values-driven program.

Kelsey speaks first from his Extraverted function, which is his auxiliary decision-making Thinking function. He is concerned that the order of the agenda makes sense, that it be logical. Later he uses his dominant Introverted Sensing to reflect on the new information Vanessa gives him. He examines and ponders the information until he integrates it with his previous thoughts.

When Kelsey speaks again, it is also from his Extraverted Thinking function. But this time, he has processed and internalized Vanessa's information so thoroughly that he has made it his own. Vanessa, of course, does not hear Kelsey's thought process. She hears only the decision Kelsey has made.

APPLYING TYPE: *What a listener does not hear.* Communication sometimes involves surprises such as a change of mind. Type dynamics helps us recognize that what seems like a sudden change of mind often is the product of the unheard and unseen action of the Introverted function.

People who have a preference for Judging and extravert Thinking or Feeling tend to speak first from this Extraverted decision-making function. Statements often sound decisive and final. A listener may assume that a decision is already made and new information will not be heard or welcomed. The listener may later be surprised, however, to hear a new decision—a change of mind—based on information the listener thought was unheard.

A person who wishes to have another person consider new information may find it most effective to offer the information and then let it go, not expecting an immediate response. The original speaker may actually hear the information, reflect on it with the Introverted information-gathering function (Sensing or Intuition), and then make a new decision based on the seemingly dismissed information.

The listener does not hear the Introverted reflection process. The listener only hears the Extraverted decision-making process that results in both the original decision and the new decision.

Kelsey's unheard Introverted Sensing function becomes apparent once we analyze his type and listen to what he says. The role of Vanessa's Introverted

Feeling function is not so apparent because its contribution comes in what she does not say. A common reaction from someone in Vanessa's position might have been to say, "That's what I said in the first place." She might have added, "Why couldn't you just have made this decision in the meeting? I've spent two days trying to figure out what to do, when you could have saved me the time and worry."

However, in this incident, Vanessa did not say these things to Kelsey. She used her Introverted Feeling function to evaluate possible responses to Kelsey's new decision. She realized that speaking her thoughts would not be helpful to her working relationship with Kelsey. She also realized that his new decision was an indication that he had heard her request, respected the values that were important to her, and accepted her suggestion for a change in the agenda.

part four out-of-pattern communication

People tend to begin communication by speaking from the Extraverted function, the part of the personality that others typically see first. In everyday casual conversation, it is likely the communication mode people use most often.

At times, language does not fit our expectations. Communication surprises us because it is "out of pattern." Such communication is not abnormal behavior, but it does reflect functions that have become exaggerated in specific situations. We may recognize out of pattern communication when a person (a) speaks not from the expected Extraverted function but from the Introverted function or (b) speaks from an exaggerated function.

Part 4 looks at communication from the Introverted function and at the exaggerated use of a function, and ends with a discussion of constructive use of type differences.

"With the current stress levels in organizations, it is our experience that many people are in type exaggeration much of the time."

Nancy J. Barger and Linda K. Kirby,
The Challenge of Change in Organizations:
Helping Employees Thrive in the New Frontier

chapter 10 speaking from the introverted function

When a person suddenly speaks from an Introverted function, communication may seem out of pattern. Passion about an interest or concern is a common stimulus for speaking from the Introverted function. Sometimes stress spurs such a response. This chapter offers examples of both scenarios.

Passion and the Introverted Function

A topic about which a person is passionate or has a compelling interest or concern can be a stimulus for speaking from the Introverted Function. A passionate interest in a topic typically reflects personal values and experiences more than type preferences. Type preferences are more likely to influence how the passion is expressed or acted upon.

Signs of an Introverted Function Influenced by Passion

When passion influences an individual to speak from the Introverted function, a listener may observe one or more of the following characteristics.

- The person speaks louder, faster, and with more animation than is typical.
- The speaker seems disengaged from the conversation.
  - The person seems to be speaking aloud to himself or herself in the presence of others rather than speaking to or with others.
- The person speaks very softly.

Most people have one or more interests about which they are passionate. If a person's passion is associated with an Extraverted function, we are likely to accept that person's expression of the passion as typical and natural for that individual. When a person's passion is associated with an Introverted function, however, we may experience the person's expression of the passion as out of character for that individual. No matter whether the person introverts the dominant function or the auxiliary function, when the passion bursts forth, we hear the communication and see the actions of that individual as out of pattern.

Introverted Dominant Function Speaks Out

Type theory describes typical characteristics and patterns of behavior, not rigid rules. This principle may be particularly evident in the speech of Introverted types, whose dominant functions and primary communication modes are different functions. A typical characteristic is that a person generally speaks from the Extraverted function. However, this is not a rigid rule. For example, the dominant function has a powerful influence on the expression of type. When passion engages the dominant function, a person who has a preference for Introversion may speak directly from the Introverted dominant function rather than from the more expected Extraverted function.

The following stories illustrate the influence of passion on the Introverted dominant function.

Dominant Introverted Intuition (N_I): Rusty

Rusty (INTJ) was asked to participate in a specific aspect of a research project. His face lit up and his first response was, "Let me suggest other possibilities or ways I can be of help to you."

 LISTENING FOR TYPE CLUES. Consider the type dynamics and communication functions for an INTJ:

Type Dynamics		Communication	
Dominant function	N_I	Primary function	T_E
Auxiliary function	T_E	Secondary function	N_I
Third function	F	Third function	F
Fourth function	S_E	Fourth function	S_E

Rusty's primary communication function is Extraverted Thinking. According to type and communication theories, we might expect Rusty's first response to reflect the auxiliary Thinking function. For example, he might dispassionately begin, "I presume you have . . . ," and state procedures that he considers important. This could give him a way to critique the project before committing to it. However, research is Rusty's interest, his occupation, and his passion. When he was asked to participate in a research project, the request immediately engaged Rusty's passion so that his first response was, "Let me suggest other possibilities or ways I can be of help to you." The passion triggered a response from the dominant Introverted Intuition function.

Dominant Introverted Sensing (S_I): Marvin

Marvin (ISFJ) received a list from a contractor of supplies available for a project. He disappeared into his cubicle for some time. When he emerged, he bubbled with excitement.

> **Marvin:** I created a spreadsheet by scanning all the prices in the list. I scanned it into WordPerfect®, then converted it to RTF, then opened it as a Works word processing document, then converted it into a spreadsheet. I probably could have scanned it into an RTF document to start with, but the scanner software is programmed to scan into WordPerfect. I wanted to be able to group items and get subtotals.

 LISTENING FOR TYPE CLUES. The type dynamics and communication functions for Marvin's type, ISFJ, look like this:

Type Dynamics		Communication	
Dominant function	S_I	Primary function	F_E
Auxiliary function	F_E	Secondary function	S_I
Third function	T	Third function	T
Fourth function	N_E	Fourth function	N_E

According to theories of type and communication, we might expect to hear Marvin speak from the Extraverted Feeling function. In most everyday conversation, we would likely hear him use personal words to speak of cooperation between work associates, as well as about materials that support people involved in a mutual project. For example, he might tell a co-worker, "The contractor sent us the list of available supplies, so now we can get what we need for our project." Instead, Marvin gives a detailed account of the steps he took to process data. For him data is information. Step-by-step development of a spreadsheet provides a way to manipulate the data so that he can extract desired information from it. These characteristics are associated with Introverted Sensing, his dominant function.

In this incident, Marvin appears to have a passion for the project. The receipt of relevant data engages his dominant Introverted Sensing function. He seeks ways to make the list of facts useful in a practical way so that he can apply the information to the project. Achieving the goal excites him with a sense of satisfaction and accomplishment, which he wants to share. His passion leads him to speak directly from his Introverted Sensing function, and results in behavior that his co-workers rarely witness.

Introverted Auxiliary Function Speaks Out

Sometimes passion is so powerful that it prompts even the Introverted auxiliary function to speak out. The story that follows illustrates out-of-pattern communication resulting from use of the Introverted auxiliary function.

Auxiliary Introverted Feeling (F_I): Heather

Heather (ESFP) is the caregiver for her mother, Georgia. Dr. Allen, Georgia's physician, appreciates that Heather accompanies her mother on medical visits because he knows Heather pays attention to his directions for care. Esther is a nurse in Dr. Allen's clinic.

> Dr. Allen: How are you two today?
>
> Heather: Can't complain. Wouldn't do any good if I did. How was your trip? Esther said you were gone for ten days.
>
> Dr. Allen: It was a good medical conference. What brings you in today?
>
> Heather: Mother's had five mini-strokes in the last three weeks.
>
> Dr. Allen: First we'd need to monitor you, Georgia, to see how often they occur, whether they come under particular conditions. As you know, what the average person calls a mini-stroke is actually a TIA—Transient Ischemic Attack.

Heather: They're more frequent now. I didn't think too much about it when Mother had one Wednesday afternoon three weeks ago at 1:30. Then she had two the next week—Tuesday at about 2:10 in the afternoon, and Friday morning just after breakfast. This week she's already had two—Monday afternoon about 3:20, and Wednesday morning, that time during breakfast.

Dr. Allen: What we want to watch for is—

Heather: Look at her.

Dr. Allen: Yes. The symptoms are—

Heather: Stop talking. Look at her. See that? Her right eyelid just drooped. The right side of her mouth is sagging.

Dr. Allen: How are you feeling, Georgia?

Heather: She can't answer you now. See her eyes? They're glazed. This isn't a schoolbook. This is real. She's having a mini-stroke right now. She's your schoolbook now. Don't tell me what to look for. Tell me what we're going to do.

Dr. Allen: (later that day, to Esther) I saw a side of Heather today I've never seen before. She's usually easygoing, but it was like a hard side of her came out today.

LISTENING FOR TYPE CLUES. The type dynamics for ESFPs look like this:

Type Dynamics		Communication	
Dominant function	S_E	Primary function	S_E
Auxiliary function	F_I	Secondary function	F_I
Third function	T	Third function	T
Fourth function	N_I	Fourth function	N_I

Heather has a combination of Sensing and Feeling preferences. She tends to pay attention to people-related details—for example, the name of the nurse and the doctor's ten-day absence. Her Sensing function is Extraverted, giving her a focus on practical reality as illustrated by such comments as "wouldn't do any good to complain" and by her attention to the number, day, and time of each TIA incident, as well as to the signs of a TIA in progress. Most of the time, Heather observes these details in a matter-of-fact way.

Heather's Extraverted Sensing function is both her dominant function and her primary communication function. Her doctor is used to communication influenced by Extraverted Sensing.

However, when through Extraverted Sensing, Heather notices signs of a TIA in progress, and she determines that the doctor does not observe the signs, she becomes passionate and suddenly speaks from her auxiliary Introverted Feeling function.

According to type and communication theories, Feeling for ESFPs is a secondary function in every way. Feeling is the

- auxiliary function;
- Introverted function;
- secondary communication function.

Introverted Feeling defines and protects core values by which a person lives. So Heather quickly expresses her auxiliary Introverted Feeling function when she feels that the doctor pays insufficient attention to details about her mother's health—a concern about which she is passionate. Heather is incensed that Dr. Allen remains in a teaching rather than a teachable mode when her mother shows symptoms of a TIA. With her passion engaged, Heather switches her mode of speaking from Extraverted Sensing to Introverted Feeling, a mode Dr. Allen has not seen Heather put into action.

Stress and the Introverted Function

Stress is sometimes a stimulus for speaking from the Introverted function. When we observe type characteristics of people under stress, we may see people communicate from the Introverted function when stress is mild. If stress is acute or prolonged, we are more likely to see people exaggerate the use of a function, which is an out-of-pattern behavior discussed in the next chapter. The following story illustrates speaking from the Introverted function when a person is under mild stress.

Introverted Feeling (F$_I$): Grayson

Grayson (INFP) is a psychologist who conducts daylong workshops about once a week to train hospice volunteers on grief issues. He also sees clients two days a week at a clinic and teaches one course one day a week at a nearby university. Grayson values pacing himself so that he can do his best work in each setting. However, recently he has received a number of requests for his workshops. To accommodate the requests, he agreed to do four workshops in four different cities during a weeklong university break. The facilitator of the fourth workshop gave the following report to a colleague.

> We were looking forward to having Grayson come. He's been here before, and the volunteers always appreciate his caring, his depth of understanding of issues, and his leadership style. He's been good at getting people to participate actively in the sessions. He's encouraged the volunteers to consider options for various scenarios and has helped them practice needed skills.
>
> This workshop was different, though. Oh, the morning session was fine, but the afternoon was a disappointment. According to the outline Grayson gave us, he was going to give a brief introduction to a concept and then have us work in small groups with case studies and related questions. But he never did get us into groups or let us discuss the questions. He just read each study and answered the questions himself. I know he gave some answers the volunteers might not have considered, but I don't think they heard his insights. Grayson seemed oblivious to the few people who tried to ask questions or make comments. Sometimes his voice was so soft we could scarcely hear him, and after a while, some people even dozed off, but he didn't seem to notice. He didn't really seem awake himself. You've heard of sleepwalking. Well, he seemed to be "sleeptalking."
>
> I've talked with the coordinators of the first three workshops, and they said Grayson did fine. Next time he does a tour, I'll insist that he come here on the first or second day, not the last day.

 LISTENING FOR TYPE CLUES. The type dynamics and communication functions for an INFP look like this:

Type Dynamics		Communication	
Dominant function	F_I	Primary function	N_E
Auxiliary function	N_E	Secondary function	F_I
Third function	S	Third function	S
Fourth function	T_E	Fourth function	T_E

Grayson usually leads workshops through his primary communication function of Extraverted Intuition. Based on past experience, the workshop facilitator expected that Grayson would give brief introductions to material and let participants discuss case studies. She expected that he would encourage the volunteers to generate ideas and to practice skills they could use with their hospice patients.

The facilitator found Grayson's extended lecture out of character for him. Although he was speaking aloud, he seemed to be talking more to himself than to the people before him. In fact, he behaved as if he were scarcely aware that other people were present.

The content of Grayson's lecture relates to a people-centered issue, consistent with the characteristics of his dominant Introverted Feeling function. Directing his people-centered focus toward issues in hospice care likely is due to personal interests. In some settings, Grayson probably speaks from the Introverted Feeling function because he becomes passionate about his topic. In the current setting, however, Grayson appears to be fatigued, as he speaks with little or no passion.

For a person who prefers Introversion, as Grayson does, the Extraverted activity of communication requires extra energy, especially when the communication is with a group of people. Grayson expended this energy for several days while on a schedule that was strenuous for him. By the afternoon of the fourth day, he had depleted his Extraversion energy. Although Grayson was not consciously aware of doing so, he mentally retreated from his Extraverted function to his more comfortable Introverted Feeling function, where he could relieve some of his stress and study his topic in the sanctuary of inner quiet and solitude.

APPLYING TYPE: *Using functions one at a time.* Isabel Myers said that people need to use each function as appropriate, but that they cannot use two functions at exactly the same time. However, sometimes people switch from one function to another in a nanosecond. For example, a person may use the perception function Sensing to notice that there is a glare on the page, and immediately switch to a judgment function—perhaps Thinking—to decide that moving the angle of the page would reduce the glare. Or a person may have a preference for Intuition, but quickly turn it off temporarily to give attention to specific facts and details.

Under the stress of fatigue, Grayson turned off Extraverted activity for a while and withdrew into the comfort zone of his Introverted Feeling function.

the art of dialogue

He was sufficiently aware that he was still standing before a group that he continued to speak, but he was no longer in dialogue with the group. One observer described his behavior by saying it was as if Grayson were reading a text printed on the inside of his eyelids rather than seeing the people in front of him. He was speaking his internal thoughts from his Introverted Feeling function.

chapter 11 exaggerated use of a function

When a person speaks from an exaggerated use of a function, communication may seem out of pattern. Exaggeration is likely to occur most often in one of the following situations.

- A person is stressed or fatigued.
- There is a lack of type development or a person is in the midst of type development.

In cases of exaggerated use of a function, we may observe characteristics such as the following.

- Speech seems out of control for the situation.
- Language may not match actions.
- Communication seems one-sided or disrupted.
- There is a lack of natural balance between perception (information gathering) and judgment (evaluation and decision making).
- One function is overused in inappropriate and extreme ways.

Consequences of Overuse of a Function

Psychological type, as described by Jung, and Myers and Briggs, identifies natural personality differences between people. Descriptions of psychological type assume appropriate use of preferences, but the theory also accounts for patterns that are typical when expressions of type are not optimal.

Typical patterns of inappropriate use of preferences are apparent when a function becomes exaggerated. A number of authors, including Barger and Kirby (1995), Hirsh and Kummerow (1998), and Quenk (2000, 2002), have identified characteristics of exaggerated functions. These characteristics of exaggerated use of the four functions may result in behaviors such as the following.

Sensing: Rather than giving accurate attention to facts and details, the person becomes obsessed with inconsequential or impractical details. Rather than finding pleasure in experiences that engage the senses, the person overindulges in sensual pleasure or withdraws from sensual pleasure.

Intuition: Rather than having visionary insight or optimism about the future, the person fantasizes grandiose ideas or catastrophic results.

Thinking: Rather than using logical analysis, searching for truth, or taking decisive action, the person employs convoluted logic or aggressive criticism, or takes precipitous action.

Feeling: Rather than being comfortable sharing emotions and being sensitive to the welfare of others, the person has emotional outbursts or becomes hypersensitive.

We know from type theory that each personality type has its own set of strengths. However, all types are vulnerable to overuse of these strengths. When strengths are carried to extremes, they can become liabilities. Such overuse, no matter what form it takes, typically results in a breakdown of communication.

Stress and Exaggerated Functions

Any function may be used in an exaggerated way. In times of stress, however, the hierarchical order of the functions seems to influence which functions a person is most likely to exaggerate. Often the exaggerated function is either the dominant or the inferior (fourth) function. The stories that follow are examples of exaggerated use of a function in times of stress.

An Exaggerated Fourth (Inferior) Function: Susan

As described in chapter 7, several terms are used to name the fourth function. The term *inferior function* is usually most descriptive when a person is under

the art of dialogue

stress. In these times, the fourth function seizes control of the personality so that the person's behaviors appear primitive and childish.

Another way to describe what happens under stress is to say that a person falls into the inferior function. The hierarchy of the functions (discussed in chapter 7) places the functions in an order for each type:

1) Dominant function
2) Auxiliary function
3) Third function
4) Fourth/inferior function.

People tend to progress through the order in type development but not when they are under stress. A person under severe or acute stress is likely to plummet from the dominant function directly to the inferior function. The person does a free fall from the solid ground of the best-developed function to the quicksand of the least-developed function. The following story is an example of the effects of falling into the inferior function in a time of acute stress.

Susan (ISFJ) is office manager in a shopping mall anchor store in a midsize city. The store is part of a regional chain. Susan is a single parent of a fifteen-year-old son and a twelve-year-old daughter. One morning Susan telephoned an employment counselor requesting an immediate appointment.

> Susan: I need a new job right away. I've been awake all night trying to think how to find one. Yesterday, just at quitting time, the manager called all the employees together and told us our chain of stores was sold to another regional chain. Just like that! It's in today's newspaper. The buyer already has stores at the other two malls in our city, so I know they'll close our store. Even if they keep it open, they'll bring in their own people. Either way I'll lose my job. I won't be able to make my mortgage payment. I saved five years to make the down payment, and now I'll lose the house. I won't be able to put money into the kids' college accounts. I'll have to go on food stamps. The court will think I can't provide for my kids, and I'll lose custody. If I don't get a job right away, I'll lose everything I've worked so hard to get. I just want to cry, but I'm too angry to cry. There's so much to do, I don't know where to start. You've got to help me.

LISTENING FOR TYPE CLUES. The type dynamics for Susan's personality type, ISFJ, look like this:

Dominant function	S_I	Perception (information-gathering)
Auxiliary function	F_E	Judgment (decision-making)
Third function	T	Judgment (decision-making)
Fourth/inferior function	N_E	Perception (information-gathering)

Under stress, Susan falls into her inferior Extraverted Intuition function. She does not use Extraverted Intuition in its developed, appropriate way of seeing possibilities. Instead, she moves from one unlikely probability to the next and quickly comes to conclusions about improbabilities. Such characteristics are an expression of Extraverted Intuition erupting out of control when a person is under stress.

APPLYING TYPE: *Falling into the inferior function.* Typically a function, when used in an exaggerated way, shuts out the operation of other functions. Under such circumstances, communication becomes difficult. If Susan's employment counselor knows about type and recognizes an out-of-control inferior function, the counselor's first reaction might be to attempt to speak to Susan's dominant function. The dominant function, after all, is the unifying force of the personality and is in charge when an individual is operating at that person's best. However, type experts suggest that when a person has fallen into the inferior function, it is often more helpful to attempt to speak to the auxiliary or third function.

Looking at type dynamics helps us understand this advice. In the dynamics chart shown earlier for Susan's type, we notice two things about the relationship between the dominant and inferior functions.

- Both the dominant and inferior functions are from the same fundamental mental process.
- In the hierarchical order of the functions, the dominant and inferior functions are the greatest distance apart.

As we see in Susan's chart, both her dominant Sensing function and her inferior Intuition function are from the same fundamental mental process, perception, which is used for information gathering. If the counselor attempts to move Susan from the inferior function directly to the dominant function, she will ask Susan to go from the possibilities of Intuitive information to the facts of Sensing information. But at the moment, Susan is not using any kind of information well. She sees every fact as a catastrophic possibility.

Further, as described earlier, in the hierarchy of functions the dominant and inferior functions are the greatest distance apart. Under acute stress, a person may plummet from the number one dominant function directly to the number four inferior function. However, returning from the inferior function directly to the dominant function generally is not so easy as a simple long leap. Another strategy is needed. For that, we turn to other functions in the hierarchy.

Speaking to the auxiliary or third function alleviates both problems that arise from the relationship of the dominant and inferior functions. If we look again at the type dynamics chart for Susan, we see the following additional information.

- The auxiliary and third functions are from the opposite fundamental process of the dominant and inferior functions.
- The distance between the fourth position and the second or third position is shorter than the distance between the fourth and first position.

In the hierarchy of functions, the auxiliary and third functions are from one fundamental process, while the dominant and inferior functions are from the other fundamental process. For Susan, her auxiliary and third functions of Feeling and Thinking are both judgment (decision-making) processes. If Susan is stuck in inappropriate use of the perception process, the counselor can attempt to get her to shift gears to the judgment process. A first step might be simply to listen in an empathetic way. In doing so, the counselor may be able to help Susan move toward her auxiliary Extraverted Feeling function by affirming the relationships and values Susan names—her relationship with her children and her values of owning her house and working hard. The counselor may also be able to help Susan access her Thinking function by beginning to analyze a few of the catastrophic possibilities Susan names. How likely is it that Susan will not be able to make the next mortgage payment? How likely is it that she will lose her house if she misses one payment?

Further, in the hierarchy of functions, the distance is shorter between the fourth and the second or third positions than between the fourth and first positions. While a person is likely to plummet from the first to the fourth function when under acute stress, the way back out of the inferior function is more likely to be a climb through the hierarchy. The second and third functions can be supports that aid the person in climbing back to the dominant function.

Some type experts are even more specific and would suggest that the counselor first attempt to speak to the third function. The third function may be flexible in attitude and can most easily be used in either an Extraverted or Introverted way. (See chapter 7 for the discussion on three theories about the attitude of the third function.) This flexibility may be one more available tool for the counselor to use to attempt to establish communication with Susan.

An Exaggerated Dominant Function: Derek

A typical common assumption is that when a person is under stress, he or she expresses that stress through the fourth or inferior function. However, type experts have found that this assumption does not always hold true. In the following story, Derek exaggerates the dominant function.

Derek (INFJ) is director of a performing arts center. The center has seen declining revenue and increasing expenses in each of the past three years. Until now, reserves from gifts and grants have been used to continue previous levels of programming. Now the reserves are nearly gone and sources for grants are disappearing. At its last meeting, the board brainstormed possible short-term solutions: cutting back office hours, cutting the number of performances in a season, and renegotiating with the artists' agency for young but up-and-coming artists. The board asked Derek to write a proposal to deal with the financial problem. Here, Derek presents his plan to the board.

> **Derek:** At our last meeting, we started envisioning plans for the future. I'm excited about the ideas in the materials you have in your hands. This plan expands the audience we can reach. We already have artists under contract for public performances. We can bring schoolchildren and their teachers and parents to our center for special performances. Our mission statement says we are here to serve the whole community. With this new program, we can reach families that are not our usual patrons. The chart shows an implementation plan. The first year we'll choose a few schools in which to pilot the program. Then we can expand it to all city schools the second year and to county schools the third year. Just imagine the impact we can have on children! It will be publicity for our center. We can put our city on the cultural arts map.
>
> **Board member 1:** A project this ambitious would take a lot of staff time, and our staff is already fully scheduled. Who would do this?
>
> **Board member 2:** Do we know that artists are willing to add extra performances to their contracts?

Board member 3: Have schools asked for this program? Who would be responsible for transporting children between the schools and the center? How many parents could or would attend such programs?

Board member 4: I don't see any cost projections. How many new people could be expected to become paying patrons?

Board member 5: We're in a financial crisis. I don't see that this proposal has anything to do with the financial problems we already have.

Derek: These questions get into details. I really believe this is a way to live our mission statement, not just have words on paper. If the board endorses this proposal, we can work out the details.

 LISTENING FOR TYPE CLUES. The type dynamics of Derek's personality type, INFJ, look like this:

Dominant function	N_I	Perception (information-gathering)
Auxiliary function	F_E	Judgment (decision-making)
Third function	T	Judgment (decision-making)
Fourth/inferior function	S_E	Perception (information-gathering)

The financial problems have been going on for three years, so Derek has been working in a stressful environment for quite some time. Under stress, Derek exaggerates the use of his dominant Introverted Intuition function. Stimulated by the board's request to bring a proposal to the members and with his own interest in the goals of the mission statement, he gives his imagination free rein to develop a plan for expanded performances to schoolchildren.

The board expected Derek to state and analyze costs realistically and to decide ways to cut costs. These tasks typically engage Sensing and Thinking functions, neither of which are type preferences for Derek. Under stress, Derek avoids using his less-preferred functions and exaggerates use of his type preferences.

APPLYING TYPE: *Getting unstuck.* In their book *The Challenge of Change in Organizations*, Nancy Barger and Linda Kirby (1995) show that different levels of stress may affect different expressions of type. At one level of stress, the dominant function may take over the personality and show itself in an exaggerated way. At another level of stress, the inferior function may take over.

Derek's behavior exemplifies the former reaction. He exaggerates his dominant function, Intuition. Board members attempt to dialogue with Derek through a series of questions, most asking for data associated with the Sensing function. However, if Derek is stuck in exaggerated use of his dominant Intuition function, it is unlikely he will effectively use his least-preferred Sensing function to answer the board's queries. As we can see in the chart of type dynamics for Derek, both Intuition and Sensing are perception (information-gathering) functions. In his current state of mind, Derek does not use either perception function well.

If a board member knows about type and recognizes Derek's use of the exaggerated Intuition function, the board member could attempt to establish dialogue by speaking to the auxiliary Feeling function, which is a judgment (decision-making) function. Derek uses that function when he focuses on a value in the mission statement—the organization's mandate to serve the whole community. The board member could attempt to bring Derek back to the Feeling function by reminding him of the value of the performing arts center, and focusing on a mutual desire to keep the center open. The board member could emphasize what currently works and brings in revenue. This change of focus might interrupt the runaway Intuition function so that Derek and the board members could hold an effective discussion of the problem at hand.

Type Development and Exaggerated Functions

We often see exaggerated use of functions during the course of type development. As each new function develops, we may observe exaggerated use of the function for a period of time.

The hierarchical order of functions identifies the typical progression of type development. In general, very young children use functions in random order, but by the time they are approximately school age, they begin to focus on purposeful use of one function—the dominant function. Typically, young people begin to develop the auxiliary function in adolescence. As with physical, intellectual, social, or emotional development, psychological type development has no fixed timetable. It only follows general patterns.

One characteristic we may observe within the pattern of type development is a period of exaggerated use of the developing function. The following stories illustrate exaggerated use of functions in young people who are at different levels of type development.

An Exaggerated Dominant Function: Maria

As explained in chapter 7, balance in type dynamics means having one information-gathering perception function (Sensing or Intuition) and one decision-making judgment function (Thinking or Feeling). Balance means that the dominant function is from one process (perception or judgment) and the auxiliary function is from the other.

The following story is an example of an adolescent who appears to have development of the dominant function only. Without access to a developed auxiliary function, she uses her dominant function in an exaggerated way.

Maria, age fifteen, has had an introduction to personality type and has reported ENFP as her type. Late one evening, she bursts into the house and confronts her father.

Maria: You almost got me arrested.

Father: What are you talking about?

Maria: I was riding my bike and came to this red traffic light, and this police officer yelled at me from his car. He said he almost hit me because I didn't have a rear reflector on my bike.

Father: Not having a reflector sounds like something you'd get a warning ticket for, not arrested for.

Maria: Well, he didn't say he was arresting me, but I knew that's what he meant.

Father: He was in a patrol car, so you assumed that's what he meant.

Maria: Well, no, it was an unmarked car, but I'm sure he was a police officer.

Father: So he was in uniform, and he identified himself as a police officer.

Maria: No, he was a plainclothes officer, but I know he was a police officer, and he yelled at me.

Father: Police officers don't usually yell about something like that unless you try to run.

Maria: Well, he didn't exactly yell, but he was upset, and he said he almost didn't see me, and I need a reflector.

Father: I bought a reflector for you only three months ago. What's wrong with it? You didn't tell me it's not working.

Maria: Oh, I haven't had time to put it on yet.

Father: Where is it?

Maria: Somewhere in my room, I guess.

LISTENING FOR TYPE CLUES. Clearly, this incident involves more than psychological type. Adolescence is a time of physical, emotional, and social change and a time of establishing independence from parents. Although Maria has reported type preferences, we want to remain tentative about the identification of preferences for any person in childhood and adolescence. Still, Maria reveals clues about type preferences and stages of type development that help us understand the scenario.

Maria appears to speak almost entirely from the Intuition function and from an exaggerated overuse of it. According to her responses to her father's questioning, a man in a car told Maria she needed a reflector on her bicycle. It appears that her imagination quickly generated possibilities, and from these, she leapt to a conclusion that the man was a police officer ready to arrest her.

APPLYING TYPE: *Undeveloped preferences.* If, as Maria matures, she continues to report ENFP as her personality type, then Extraverted Intuition would be her dominant function. The type dynamics for ENFP look like this:

Dominant function	N_E	Perception (information-gathering)
Auxiliary function	F_I	Judgment (decision-making)
Third function	T	Judgment (decision-making)
Fourth function	S_I	Perception (information-gathering)

At least in this incident, it seems likely that Maria has an undeveloped auxiliary function. For a person with preferences for Extraversion, Intuition, and Perceiving, the auxiliary function is a judgment function—Thinking or Feeling. Either Thinking or Feeling, when developed and used appropriately, can provide a way to evaluate the possibilities generated by the Intuition and to make decisions about whether each possibility is rational. Maria appears to accept all the possibilities she imagines without evaluating them through either the Thinking or Feeling function. Without the balancing action of a developed auxiliary judgment function, Maria's dominant Extraverted Intuition is immature and, in a way, runs wild.

Maria's father facilitates communication by speaking the lines that Maria might if she were using a judgment (decision-making) function. In this conversation, it is as if Maria and her father are actors in a play. Maria plays the perception role (Intuition) and her father the judgment role (Thinking or Feeling). He evaluates the statements expressed through the perception function (Intuition). He does not judge her statements. Rather, he models for her what her own judgment function of Feeling could do. (Remember that in type theory, the term *judgment* refers to the way a person evaluates information and comes to a decision through use of the Thinking or Feeling function.)

The type development task for Maria as she moves through adolescence is to use her auxiliary function in a purposeful and appropriate way. If she continues to identify ENFP as her preferences, then we would expect to observe her beginning to use the Feeling function. As she matures, we would expect to see balance between her perception function (Intuition) and her judgment function (Feeling). When she achieves skill with the auxiliary function and balance between perception and judgment, she will be less likely to exaggerate her dominant function.

An Exaggerated Auxiliary Function: Zane

As an individual progresses through type development, the person tends to exaggerate use of each function as that function becomes the focus of development. In the following conversation, we hear Zane use the auxiliary function in an exaggerated way.

Zane, age sixteen, has had an introduction to personality type and has identified ENTP as his type. He is having dinner with his family.

> **Mom:** After dinner I want you to pick up the things you left on the floor by the front door and take them to your room.
>
> **Zane:** Why? It's stuff I need in the morning. I might not see it in my room.
>
> **Mom:** Then you need to clean your room.
>
> **Zane:** Why? It'll just get messed up again.
>
> **Dad:** Zane, please pass the mashed potatoes.
>
> **Zane:** Why?

exaggerated use of a function

LISTENING FOR TYPE CLUES. The type dynamics for ENTPs, the type Zane has reported, look like this:

Dominant function	N$_E$	Perception (information-gathering)
Auxiliary function	T$_I$	Judgment (decision-making)
Third function	F	Judgment (decision-making)
Fourth function	S$_I$	Perception (information-gathering)

Keeping in mind that adolescence is a time of great change, we can still make some observations about type preferences and behavior. Zane appears to speak almost entirely from the Thinking function and from an exaggerated use of it. He responds to each statement from his parents with the question "Why?" followed by a rationale for why he has not complied. His parents may say he is giving excuses.

APPLYING TYPE: *Process of type development.* Since Zane is an adolescent and is using his Thinking preference in an unpolished way, it appears that he is in the midst of development of his auxiliary Thinking function. Type practitioners identify four stages of the development of a function, as follows:

1) random use
2) bumbling use
3) overuse
4) appropriate and integrated use.

The task of type development for adolescents is to gain skill in appropriate use of the auxiliary function. Then, they need to integrate the dominant and auxiliary functions so that they have good use of one information-gathering process (Sensing or Intuition) and one decision-making process (Thinking or Feeling).

According to the theory of type development, the dominant function typically goes through the stages of development during childhood. Parents often report that shortly before the onset of adolescence, they feel that they have a good relationship with their child and that the child really is beginning to grow up. Theory suggests that by that age, the child has reasonable mastery of the dominant function. The child is likely to be comfortable with himself, and the parents are likely to feel that they know their child.

Then, the child enters adolescence. In addition to physical and other

the art of dialogue

changes, the child also begins a new stage of type development. The auxiliary function comes to the forefront of the personality. As the stages of development indicate, the adolescent begins at the bumbling stage (having passed through the random stage in early childhood) and moves into the overuse stage. The adolescent also moves from the process and attitude of the dominant function to the opposite process and attitude of the auxiliary function.

If Zane continues to identify ENTP as his type, his dominant function—presumably developed in childhood—is a perception (information-gathering) process in the Extraverted attitude (Extraverted Intuition). In adolescence he begins to develop his auxiliary function, which is a judgment (decision-making) process in the Introverted attitude (Introverted Thinking).

Zane's behavior as illustrated in the dialogue with his parents seems to be a result of the natural type development process. At his current stage of development, he gives full attention to his auxiliary Introverted Thinking function, to the extent that he uses it in an exaggerated way. He is experimenting with a new function and a new attitude and no longer lives in the comfort zone that he knew in late childhood. His parents also see new behaviors in him and feel that they no longer know their son.

According to theory, as Zane moves through adolescence, he will progress from the overuse stage of the function to the final stage of appropriate and integrated use. By the time he reaches young adulthood, he is likely to be comfortable with himself again. His parents are likely to get to know him as the more mature person he has become. Each may even see the other as having somehow grown wiser.

chapter 12 constructive use of differences

**"

Throughout her life, Isabel Myers focused on helping people appreciate their own strengths and gifts, recognize their potential areas for growth and development, and understand valuable differences in one another. Through these efforts, she hoped to enable people to use differences constructively.

A first step to constructive use of differences is recognition of characteristics of preferences on the four dichotomies, as described in part 2 of this book. Each person has a preference for Extraversion or Introversion, Sensing or Intuition, Thinking or Feeling, and Judging or Perceiving. Individuals can identify their preferences through self-observation of typical patterns of behavior in everyday situations. An individual can also observe possible type preferences of other people and can adapt communication to speak to those preferences.

Type dynamics, explained in parts 3 and 4, help us recognize the interaction of preferences in types and differences between Extraverted and Introverted expressions of functions. Through these concepts of type dynamics, we gain greater understanding of the complex interactions of communication. Type dynamics also helps us understand communication situations in which a speaker's language does not fit our expectations and seems out of pattern.

To make optimum use of our knowledge of type and communication, we need to use type differences constructively and adapt communication appropriately so that we meet the goal of effective communication. The following two stories illustrate use of type knowledge to adapt to communication situations. In the first story, communication is less than successful because adaptation does not help meet the goal. The second story shows use of type knowledge to achieve a satisfying outcome.

Ineffective Adaptation to Type Preferences

Carmen (INFP) and Mark (ESFJ) are browsing in an antique mall. Carmen sees a crockery bowl she would like to have and shows it to Mark. As she hears Mark's response, she attempts to draw his interest by adapting her communication to his type preferences.

Carmen: Look at that crockery bowl. Isn't it beautiful? It's in such good condition. My grandmother had a bowl like that.

Mark: It's sure expensive. What would you do with it?

Carmen: What would I do with it? I don't know. It's just nice. What do you mean?

Mark: How would you use it?

Carmen: Well, it's big enough to mix dough for cookies or bread.

(On Carmen's birthday Mark beamed as Carmen opened a large package, which contained a stainless steel mixing bowl.)

Mark: It's what you said you wanted—a bowl big enough to mix dough for cookies or bread.

 LISTENING FOR TYPE CLUES. The type dynamics and communication functions for Carmen and Mark look like this:

Carmen, INFP				Mark, ESFJ			
Type Dynamics		Communication		Type Dynamics		Communication	
Dominant	F_I	Primary	N_E	Dominant	F_E	Primary	F_E
Auxiliary	N_E	Secondary	F_I	Auxiliary	S_I	Secondary	S_I
Third	S	Third	S	Third	N	Third	N
Fourth	T_E	Fourth	T_E	Fourth	T_I	Fourth	T_I

160   the art of dialogue

Carmen speaks first from her Extraverted auxiliary function of Intuition, which is her primary communication function. She moves quickly from one idea to another—beauty, condition of the bowl, and memory of her grandmother. As she speaks, it is likely that her dominant Introverted Feeling function leads her down a path inside her own mind to deeply held memories of her grandmother that go far beyond those associated with the bowl.

Mark's first words, reflecting a personal value regarding economic worth, are from his Extraverted dominant function of Feeling. With his auxiliary function of Introverted Sensing, he listens for and hears information about a practical use of the bowl.

With a desire to interest Mark in the crockery bowl, Carmen attempts to adapt her communication to his preferences. When Mark asks what she would do with the bowl, Carmen uses her Extraverted Intuition to brainstorm practical uses, attempting to appeal to his Sensing function. However, in the process, she changes the content of her message. What she really wants to communicate to Mark is that she is interested in this particular crockery bowl because it reminds her of her grandmother. The message Mark hears is that Carmen wants a large bowl to mix dough.

Carmen might have adapted her communication mode differently and also delivered her intended message if she had remembered that people who have a Sensing preference tend to take in information step by step and that those who have a Feeling preference tend to be interested in personal values. Rather than changing the content of her message to respond to uses for the bowl, she might have explained the steps that led her inside her own mind from first admiring the bowl to remembering her grandmother and then to an interest in the bowl as a keepsake rather than as a utilitarian object.

Knowledge of type theory and application of the theory to communication are helpful when we use them to deliver a message effectively. Carmen's adaptation of her communication mode to Mark's type preferences was not helpful because she lost the content of her message in the process of the adaptation. If she had used type differences constructively, she could have had a tool to help her communicate the intended message effectively.

Constructive Adaptation to Type Preferences

Marcella (ENFJ) is a volunteer on the board of a neighborhood community center. She wants to present an idea for a fundraiser, but she knows that if her idea sounds too vague to other board members, they may not even discuss it. Kirby (INTP) is also a board member and one who often asks questions. Both Marcella and Kirby know about type and are aware of the type preferences of the other. Marcella describes her approach in preparing to present her idea to the board.

Kirby and I have known each other for several years. If I have an idea and just start talking about it with him, he has questions I can't answer, and I get upset. I find that my best avenue for communicating with him is through writing a letter. I go inside myself and put on my best thinking cap and appeal to his logic. I am successful most of the time, but I am usually very tired afterwards, and sometimes my logic is not so clear to him. However, he appreciates my effort and is often the one who approaches me to discuss the idea.

After I sent him a letter about my fundraising idea, he telephoned me. He's really quite adept at asking me questions about my perspective. I said in my letter that my goal is to bring people together and to build support for the center's tutoring program. I said that my reason for the project is my belief that if the community is involved in raising funds, they are more likely to use the program. When Kirby telephoned, he asked how I plan to involve the community, and I named the teams we will need for the project. He asked how I will recruit people, how community members will have a voice so that they feel ownership of the project, but also how the board will retain control to meet its obligations of oversight of center activities. I appreciate Kirby's interest in my idea and feel he will support a good discussion among board members.

LISTENING FOR TYPE CLUES. Marcella and Kirby use their knowledge of psychological type so that each adapts communication to the preferences of the other. Their type dynamics and communication functions look like this:

Marcella, ENFJ				Kirby, INTP			
Type Dynamics		Communication		Type Dynamics		Communication	
Dominant	F_E	Primary	F_E	Dominant	T_I	Primary	N_E
Auxiliary	N_I	Secondary	N_I	Auxiliary	N_E	Secondary	T_I
Third	S	Third	S	Third	S	Third	S
Fourth	T_I	Fourth	T_I	Fourth	F_E	Fourth	F_E

When Marcella wants to communicate with Kirby, she recognizes that using her usual communication mode of Extraverted Feeling is not an effective starting point. Extraverted Feeling is both her primary communication function and her dominant function, but it is Kirby's fourth function. Marcella also appears to know from her years of acquaintance with Kirby that when he hears her idea, he will quickly begin to evaluate the plan with his dominant Introverted Thinking function. If she is to receive Kirby's support for a discussion by the board, she needs to engage the interest of his dominant Introverted Thinking, which means she must use her fourth function to communicate with him.

Marcella supports her fourth function of Introverted Thinking by using her auxiliary Introverted Intuition to consider the kinds of questions Kirby is likely to ask and also to formulate the most logical answers she can give. She even uses the Introverted attitude of her Intuition and Thinking functions by working out her answers in writing.

Kirby recognizes Marcella's effort to adapt to his type preferences, and he makes an equal effort to adapt his communication to her preferences. After he processes her written communication with his Introverted Thinking, he adjusts to her Extraversion preference by initiating a conversation. He directs his initial questions to her dominant Extraverted Feeling function, asking about those parts of the plan that will impact people.

Marcella appreciates Kirby's questions. Sometimes people who have a Feeling preference regard questions, such as those that Kirby asks, as criticism. Marcella accurately recognizes that such questions from a person who prefers Thinking are usually expressions of interest in the idea.

Neither Marcella nor Kirby access the Sensing function during their inter-actions, but having considered Marcella's proposal through Intuition, Thinking, and Feeling, the two of them are well positioned to discuss questions raised by board members who see the Sensing perspective.

Marcella and Kirby both make constructive use of type differences. Each adapts communication to the preferences of the other. Each attempts to view the proposal from the perspective of the other. Together they revise the proposal so that by the time Marcella brings it to the board, it is strong enough to withstand a rigorous discussion.

Principles for the Constructive Use of Type

Isabel Myers's concept of the constructive use of differences can lead to improved relationships and communication. This concept is the foundation of all of the theory of type preferences and type dynamics. After delving into the component parts and complexities of type theory as we have done in this book, we need to remind ourselves of the basic principles for the constructive use of type:

- Each type is valuable.
- Each type has its own strengths and gifts.
- There are no good or bad types.
- The first purpose of type is to understand oneself.
- There are no right or wrong combinations of type in relationships or communication.
- Each person has type biases related to that person's pattern of strengths and weaknesses. Being aware of one's own biases helps avoid negative stereotyping of others.
- Each type has a natural path for lifelong development of type.

People who pay attention to the principles of constructive use of differences find that type provides a way to enhance relationships and communication through appreciation of individual differences. People who successfully apply knowledge about type preferences and type dynamics for effective relationships and communication achieve Isabel Myers's goal of constructive use of differences.

part five language in type and communication

People who say good communication has occurred usually mean the sender of the message has (a) listened to the receiver's wants and needs, (b) used the receiver's preferred method of communication, (c) provided the information most important to the receiver first, and (d) probably used words the receiver tends to use.

People of different types sometimes use the same word but with different meanings. Among words with similar meanings, different types may choose different words. Chapter 13 presents examples of both.

Type looks simple but is based on complex psychological constructs. Chapter 14 highlights a few language principles for talking about type.

Learning to listen to and speak the language of type is a lifelong process. This section offers some suggestions to help you along the way.

"Relationships are developed and sustained
through effective communication. Effective communication
demands adjustment."

Flavil R. Yeakley, Jr.,
Article in *Research in Psychological Type*

chapter 13 type and the use of language

Two people sometimes use the same word, but if asked to define the word, they would give different definitions. Other times, two words have similar meanings, but one person consistently chooses to use one of the words, and another person consistently chooses to use the other word. Observations and studies of communication suggest that type preferences influence definitions and word choices.

In this chapter, we see examples of both use of different definitions and different word choices. Although these examples are in no way exhaustive, they may raise awareness of the influence of type in the use of language.

Same Words, Different Meanings

The following examples feature some commonly used words that take on different meanings for different types. They illustrate how people often use the same words and phrases and still misunderstand one another.

Fair

People who prefer Thinking and those who prefer Feeling both speak about being fair, but they generally have different definitions for the word. People who prefer Thinking tend to define *fair* as "treating all people as equals, being objective, and avoiding favoritism." People who prefer Feeling tend to define *fair* as "treating each person as an individual, considering the circumstances of a particular situation, and leaving room for exceptions to the general rule."

Long Time/Short Time

Views of what constitutes a long time or a short time differ depending on which alternative of the Extraversion-Introversion and the Sensing-Intuition dichotomies a person prefers. For example, a comfortable period of silence tends to be longer for an Introvert than for an Extravert. The Introvert may be just at the point of getting into reflection on an idea when the Extravert becomes so uncomfortable that the he or she breaks the silence to move the communication along. The Introvert may see the resumption of conversation as a distraction that impedes the flow of thought, and therefore breaking the silence hinders rather than promotes communication. While the difference in time seems considerable to both Extraverts and Introverts, in actuality, the difference may be only a matter of seconds.

Sensing and Intuition also play a role in views about length of time. For example, sometimes in a meeting, a leader distributes a page-long proposal and gives time for group members to read it silently before discussion begins. In such a situation the allotted time is likely to seem long to those who prefer Intuition and short to those who prefer Sensing. Those who prefer Intuition are likely to scan the document, focusing on a few key words and phrases to comprehend the concept; then they may shuffle papers or drum their fingers until the reading time ends. Those who prefer Sensing are likely to read every word and may not finish in the allotted time.

The exception to the generalization about reading and time occurs when the content of a document is specific and detailed factual information, and the task is to verify the information or remember the facts. In such a situation, those who prefer Sensing are likely to complete the reading in a shorter time than those who prefer Intuition. People who have an Intuition preference and focus on key concepts tend to need a longer time to absorb facts. People who prefer Sensing tend to pick out key facts more quickly.

The time difference related to reading approaches is of particular importance in intelligence and achievement testing. These measures generally test for comprehension of concepts more than for comprehension of facts, and the tests are usually timed—factors that favor Intuition over Sensing. Research consistently shows higher mean scores on intelligence and achievement tests for students who prefer Intuition than for those who prefer Sensing.

the art of dialogue

APPLYING TYPE: *Processing time.* If in general those who prefer Extraversion or Intuition see an allotted length of time as a long time and those who prefer Introversion or Sensing see it as a short time, we can wonder whether there are cumulative effects as we combine the preferences. Gordon Lawrence (1993) cites a study of teachers and students in class discussions. The study showed that when teachers ask questions, the students who raise their hands first tend to be those who have preferences for Extraversion and Intuition (EN), while those who are slowest to raise their hands tend to be students who have preferences for Introversion and Sensing (IS). A characteristic of Extraversion is thinking aloud, while a characteristic of Introversion is reflecting before speaking. A characteristic of Intuition is trusting hunches, while a characteristic of Sensing is trusting a step-by-step, check-it-out approach.

The study found that students who have EN preferences often raise hands before they are sure of the answer, but they trust their hunches sufficiently to assume the answer will come to mind before the teacher calls on them. In contrast, students who have IS preferences tend to follow this series of steps before answering. Completing these four steps takes approximately three seconds.

1) Silently repeat to themselves the teacher's question to be sure they understand it.
2) Mentally sort through information stored in their memories to retrieve the answer.
3) Check the answer against the question to be sure it matches.
4) Raise their hands to signal readiness to respond.

The study also showed that the interval between the time a teacher finishes asking a question and calls on a student for an answer is about one second. If no student raises a hand in that interval, the teacher generally either repeats the question or rephrases it. In either case, IS students mentally check the second question against the first to be sure it is the same question and then repeat the four steps identified above. When teachers are trained to wait three seconds between asking a question and calling on a student for an answer, students who have IS preferences answer as often and as accurately as students who have EN preferences.

In actuality, a three-second wait time is a short time, especially when it provides for more equal participation between students who prefer Sensing and those who prefer Intuition. In our fast-paced culture, however, three seconds often seems like a long time. Teachers and students may need practice to become accustomed to waiting three seconds between question and response.

Frequent/Seldom

Extraverts and Introverts tend to have different definitions of *frequent* and *seldom*. Managers who have a preference for Introversion may assume that they have frequent communication with employees. In contrast, the employees who have a preference for Extraversion may say that their managers seldom communicate with them. Both may be referring to the same number of communication interactions.

For Introverts, productive work occurs in individual, quiet, and uninterrupted time. Talking with others is good for a check-in, but the talking time is not the real work time. Managers who have a preference for Introversion are likely to check in with employees, then get out of the way so the employees can get back to work.

For Extraverts, productive work occurs through talking out ideas with others. Extraverts need individual quiet time for some tasks, but when they get stuck or they complete the part of the work that has been talked through, they are likely to need another face-to-face interaction to launch the next piece of work. Employees who have a preference for Extraversion may want managers to talk with them about each new piece of work to keep the work process moving.

Large Group/Small Group

Extraverts and Introverts are likely to have different definitions for what constitutes a *large group* or a *small group*, as the following example illustrates.

Type trainers sometimes use an exercise in which they ask a group of Extraverts and a group of Introverts to plan a celebration party and to assume expense is not an issue. Extraverted participants may plan a party for fifty to one hundred people or more, often with a variety of activities. Introverted participants may plan an elaborate dinner for one to three other people.

The numbers of people chosen by each group for a celebration party is instructive. For Extraverts, a party with fifty to one hundred people is energizing. When they hear that Introverts would invite one to three other people, Extraverts may respond that the Introverts did not have a party at all. According to the Extraverts, the Introverts did not have enough people for even a small group.

the art of dialogue

For Introverts, a party with one to three people is a comfortable-sized group. Introverts sometimes use a working definition that a small group is few enough people that they can sit at a dinner table and speak one at a time and hear each other. If those at the table subdivide into conversation groups to speak and hear each other, then Introverts consider such a gathering a large group. While Introverts do not all agree on the exact number that constitutes a large group, they often define a large group as ten.

Definitions of what constitutes a small or large group become particularly important in planning social events. Because definitions have such wide variation, it may be helpful to discuss numbers rather than use the terms *large group* or *small group*.

Intelligence

For those who prefer Sensing, *intelligence* means "soundness of understanding." People who prefer Sensing tend to build a body of evidence step by step, moving from the details to a theory or conclusion. Paying attention to factual, realistic, and practical data grounds an idea on a solid foundation.

For those who prefer Intuition, *intelligence* means "quickness of understanding." People who prefer Intuition tend to start with a flash of insight, articulate it as a concept (perhaps using figurative language such as an analogy), and then begin to see some details. They attach these details to the concept until it becomes a full-blown idea or theory.

Wisdom

For people who prefer Sensing, wisdom involves learning from experience and applying that to the present. For people who prefer Intuition, wisdom involves vision, seeing beyond what is or has been and projecting into the future.

Creativity

Some lists of characteristics of personality types associate creativity only with Intuition. In actuality, both those who prefer Sensing and those who prefer Intuition demonstrate creativity, but in different ways. Marci Segal (2003) notes that creativity results from a restlessness to improve the status quo and involves generation of new ideas, use of the imagination, and decision making.

Creativity for those who prefer Intuition involves conceptual originality or developing an idea, theory, or object that has not existed before. Often the result meets a future need. Intuitive creativity is associated with many applications in the arts, with out-of-the-box strategic analysis and planning, and with research that leads to new discoveries.

Creativity for those who prefer Sensing involves adapting what is available in new ways, using something for a purpose other than what it was designed to do. It may also include crafting what is needed to be useful in a situation that has arisen suddenly or solving a long-standing challenge.

A personal experience illustrates the application of Sensing creativity. I live in a house that is more than ninety years old. Often things cannot be repaired in the typical way since nothing matches current standard measurements. However, I have been able to find carpenters, plumbers, and electricians who use Sensing creativity to solve these problems in ingenious ways.

Old recipes also exemplify the use of Sensing creativity. Stew, bread pudding, and weed soup are the result of taking what was available and creating a new food dish.

Big Picture

The phrase *big picture* has different meanings for people who prefer Intuition and for some people who prefer Sensing. People who prefer Intuition usually define big picture as "the main idea" or "the global concept." People who prefer both Sensing and Perceiving also use the phrase big picture, but they usually mean that they have gathered all the pieces and put them together into a whole.

Work Environment

The phrase *work environment* has different meanings for people with different dominant functions. An exercise that I have used for more than twenty years highlights these differences. After people have a preliminary best estimate of their personality types, I ask them to get into groups according to their dominant function. Groups have ten minutes to complete this statement: If I were in charge of the place where I work, what I would do to make it the best work environment would be . . .

Those who have Sensing as their dominant function tend to focus first on specifics in the physical environment and on the details of the job description. Those who have Intuition as their dominant function tend to start by listing many possible ways to work, and they often catalogue their desired perks. Those who have Thinking as their dominant function tend to be concerned first with guiding principles and policies. Those who have Feeling as their dominant function tend to focus first on relationships between people.

the art of dialogue

During feedback time, most participants find characteristics on the lists of other groups that they would also like in a work environment. However, in the limited time allowed to answer, the first items they bring up usually reflect the motivations of the dominant function.

When sufficiently large numbers of people make up one or more of the dominant function groups, they can be subdivided by attitude. For example, a group that has Sensing as a dominant function is divided into an Extraverted Sensing group and an Introverted Sensing group. Again, even in the short time allowed for the exercise, people tend to speak first not just from the dominant function, but also from the preferred attitude of that function.

For example, when the groups are divided into Extraverted and Introverted attitudes, Sensing groups often make clear distinctions between the physical environment around them and the structural environment that affects them as individuals. Those who prefer Extraverted Sensing tend to list elements in the physical environment, such as ergonomically designed workstations, aesthetically pleasing art and architecture that stimulates the senses, and up-to-date equipment. Those who prefer Introverted Sensing tend to list details that affect them as individuals, such as quiet space and privacy, well-defined job descriptions, clear organizational structure that tells how and where they fit in, and an employee review process.

Listening

In studies of communication reported in *Health Care Communication Using Personality Type*, Judy Allen and Susan Brock (2000) found that people of all types agree that listening is an important part of communication, but different types have different perspectives about what constitutes real listening and being heard.

Type users note that people who prefer Extraversion may feel heard as long as listeners allow the Extraverted speakers to think out loud until they come to some clarity or resolution. This process occurs primarily through the speakers' hearing their own thoughts. Sometimes Extraverts are involved in another activity while either speaking or listening. However, they remain engaged in the conversation. People who prefer Introversion may be uncomfortable in such situations and conclude that listening cannot occur while others are distracted. For Introverts, listening is likely to mean giving discernable attention to both the speaker and the topic.

Flavil Yeakley (1983) offers suggestions for listening to the "languages of the four functions"—Sensing, Intuition, Thinking, and Feeling. These suggestions appear in table 13.1 together with ways that listeners can effectively support conversations with people who speak the languages of different functions.

A useful method for a listener to employ is one that is sometimes called active listening. Listeners

- pay attention to what the speaker says;
- state what they understand the speaker to be saying;
- remain open to further clarification.

Different Words, Same Meaning

Just as people of different types may give the same word different meanings, different types sometimes select different words to represent essentially the same concept. A few examples may raise awareness of such language use.

Teacher/Mentor

Most types seem to use the word *teacher*, but people who prefer Intuition and Thinking (NT) often use *mentor* when they want to convey respect and honor. Other types do not appear to use the term mentor as part of their common vocabulary with the same frequency as do those who prefer Intuition and Thinking.

Rules/Principles/Guidelines

Different types may use different terms to designate the practices used by a group. People who have preferences for Sensing and Thinking (ST) may speak of rules, while those who prefer Intuition and Thinking (NT) are more likely to speak of principles. Those who prefer Intuition and Feeling (NF types) may speak of guidelines.

Director, Chief, Boss/Executive/Facilitator, Coordinator

Different types may select different words to refer to the leader of a group. People who have preferences for Sensing and Thinking (ST) may be comfortable with words such as *director, chief*, and *boss* that reflect hierarchy. Those who have preferences for Intuition and Thinking (NT) may choose to use the term *executive*. People who prefer Intuition and Feeling (NF) may prefer terms such as *facilitator* or *coordinator* that reflect a flat organization.

table 13.1
Suggestions for Listening to the Language of the Functions

What to Listen for in Conversation	How to Support Conversation
When the speaker prefers Sensing,	**When the speaker prefers Sensing,**
• try to hear details and facts exactly, without interrupting or rushing the speaker, and without looking for hidden messages or meanings.	• review key facts, particularly if no distinctions seem to exist between relevant facts and unimportant or unrelated details.
When the speaker prefers Intuition,	**When the speaker prefers Intuition,**
• try to hear hidden meanings and symbols, possibilities that go beyond the specific words, and dreams as well as current experiences.	• check out presumed hidden meanings or symbols before assuming you are correct in identifying them.
When the speaker prefers Thinking,	**When the speaker prefers Thinking,**
• try to hear the reasoning in what is said, the central idea, and unstated corollaries and implications.	• ask for evidence for a position or implications of an idea, particularly if the speaker appears to assume these are known and does not state them.
When the speaker prefers Feeling,	**When the speaker prefers Feeling,**
• try to hear messages of values, hopes, affections, fears, or insecurities in even simple statements.	• check out your understanding of what was said before you assume your interpretation is accurate.

Colleague/Co-worker

Different types may use different words to designate a person with whom they work. People who have preferences for Intuition and Thinking (NT) may speak of a *colleague*, while those who have preferences for Intuition and Feeling (NF) are more likely to speak of a co-worker. Definitions of the word colleague may have connotations of professional competency, an attribute especially valued by those who prefer the combination of Intuition and Thinking (NT). Definitions of the word *co-worker* tend to have connotations of relationship, an attribute especially valued by those who prefer the combination of Intuition and Feeling (NF).

In Summary

Type influences our preferences for how we communicate and what content is of interest to us. Type also influences the specific words and definitions we choose to convey the content of our communications. As we become alert to language usage, we are likely to hear many more words that have type implications.

type and the use of language

chapter 14 talking about type

When we become acquainted with the concepts of psychological type and find it useful in our own relationships and communication, we want to share our insights and interests with others. In these conversations, as in any dialogue, careful use of language is a key to conveying our messages about the benefits of type. If we are not careful with language as we talk about type, we can run into two problems.

- We can use stereotypes as we describe type.
- We can oversimplify the concepts of type.

Each problem can result in misuse of type to the detriment of others and ourselves.

This chapter presents some principles for talking about type. When we follow these principles, we join those who uphold the appropriate, ethical, and constructive use of type for the benefit of others and ourselves.

Avoiding Stereotypes

Effective communication attempts to establish understanding between a speaker and a listener and to minimize misunderstanding. Gordon Lawrence and Charles Martin (2001), in *Building People, Building Programs*, note that one source of misunderstanding about type occurs when we fail to distinguish between type and stereotype. As we become aware of type, we recognize that other people have preferences and communication patterns that are different from ours, but we view these differences through the lens of our own preferences and communication patterns. While this is natural, it can also result in our speaking in stereotypes.

A first step to avoiding stereotypes is to remember the principles developed by Isabel Myers that are the foundation for all of type theory and its applications. These basic principles are as follows:

- Each type is valuable.
- Each type has its own strengths and gifts.
- There are no good or bad types.
- The first purpose of type is to understand oneself.
- There are no right or wrong combinations of type in relationships or communication.
- Each type has a natural path for lifelong development of type.

A second step is to recognize that each of us has type biases related to our own pattern of strengths and weaknesses. Lawrence and Martin offer these suggestions to help us become aware of our own biases.

- Be alert to spots where we hear ourselves using stereotypes.
- Be aware of our own tendencies to overstate and overgeneralize, which are sources of stereotyping.
- Ask people who have preferences opposite of ours to listen for our biases and to suggest alternate, unbiased language for us to use. As we become more knowledgeable about type, we can extend this practice to those who have the same functions as ours but who express those functions in opposite attitudes.
- Continue to deepen our knowledge of type. As we have seen, there are many levels of understanding type, from basic preferences to the hierarchy of functions to the attitudes of functions to recognizing unexpected communication that seems out of pattern. A common source of stereotyping is speaking from minimal knowledge of type.

One way we can reduce stereotyping is to use language as precisely as possible. Following are four principles that can help us talk about type in language that minimizes stereotyping. Each principle includes an example of appropriate and inappropriate use of the principle.

- **Describe preferences as general tendencies rather than as specific to an individual.**

   Appropriate: People who have a preference for Intuition may prefer to . . . . *(This statement reflects a general tendency).*

   Inappropriate: You may prefer to . . . . *(This statement reflects specificity).*

When Katharine Briggs and Isabel Myers developed descriptions of the preferences and types, they named characteristics that are generally true for people who have that preference or type. However, each person is an individual, and any one characteristic may not hold true for a particular individual. When we begin a descriptive statement with the word *you*, we imply that if the person to whom we are speaking identifies with the preference, then that person must accept the particular characteristic as holding true for that person. When we use statements that begin "People who have a preference for . . . " or "People who prefer . . . ," we can avoid the stereotyping that comes with assigning a characteristic to a particular person.

- **Speak using conditional statements rather than absolute statements.**

   Appropriate: Those who prefer Sensing *may* . . . . *(This statement uses a conditional term).*

   Inappropriate: Those who prefer Sensing *will* . . . . *(This statement uses an absolute term).*

The principle about using conditional statements is related to the previous principle about describing preferences as general tendencies. Descriptions of preferences show several characteristics that are typical in most circumstances for people who have that preference. In a particular circumstance or for a particular individual, any one characteristic may not be true. When we use absolute terms such as *will, do, want,* or *like to,* we imply that the characteristic is true in all circumstances for people who have the preference we are describing. We reduce the risk of stereotyping when we use conditional words and phrases such as *tend to, often, are likely to,* and *may.*

When we begin to apply the principle of using conditional statements to our descriptions about type, we may hear ourselves being repetitive. However, the tendency of listeners to hear absolute statements is so pervasive that it is almost impossible to overuse conditional words and phrases.

- **Describe typical patterns. Avoid making an implication that a person must express a characteristic in the extreme for the characteristic to fit.**

  Appropriate: People who prefer Feeling tend to be empathetic and value harmony. *(This statement reflects typical patterns.)*

  Inappropriate: People who prefer Feeling tend to be *very* empathetic and *always* value harmony. *(This statement implies extreme patterns.)*

A general principle of effective writing is applicable to talking about type: avoid words such as *very, too, always,* and *never.* These words turn our descriptions into the overstatements and overgeneralizations that are a source of stereotyping.

- **Use descriptors that have positive connotations for people of particular preferences or types. Choose opposite terms that also have positive connotations as descriptors for people with opposite preferences or types.**

  Appropriate: Those who prefer Extraversion are often *active,* while those who prefer Introversion are more likely to be *reflective.* *(This statement includes positive descriptors.)*

  Inappropriate: Those who prefer Extraversion are often active while those who prefer Introversion are more likely to be *passive.* *(This statement includes the descriptor* passive *that tends to be interpreted in a negative way.)*

The theory of psychological type developed by Jung, and Myers and Briggs, emphasizes positive strengths. The theory accounts for weaknesses that are the opposite of strengths, but the purpose of understanding type is to value typical, natural differences among people. When she developed the MBTI® assessment tool, Isabel Myers set a goal that each item response on the assessment would be seen as desirable by the intended type. For example, if an item were on the Sensing-Intuition dichotomy, people who prefer Sensing would see the response scored toward Sensing as desirable, and people who prefer Intuition would see the response scored toward Intuition as desirable. Myers's goal was that people would be drawn to the response for their own type rather than be repelled by the response for the opposite preference.

180

Avoiding Oversimplification

When we first become acquainted with psychological type, it looks simple. Both the descriptions of preferences and the MBTI assessment tool use plain, non-technical language.

Type can be both interesting and useful even when we know only a few simple things about it. However, when we talk about type to others, we are more accurate and helpful if we understand that this seemingly simple theory and tool are actually based on complex psychological constructs. As we have seen, type is more than descriptions of a few characteristics of preferences. Extensive research has been conducted not only on the theory of type and the assessment tool but also on the language used to describe type. As we talk about type, we support the careful work that makes a complex psychological theory accessible to us when following principles that help us avoid oversimplification. Three principles are listed.

- **Identify characteristics that describe the focus or motivation of the preference or type rather than specific behaviors.**

  Appropriate: People who have a preference for Judging tend to manage their lives through organization and planning. *(This statement focuses on characteristics.)*

  Inappropriate: People who have a preference for Judging tend to have neat closets or filing cabinets and often use day planners. *(This statement focuses on behaviors.)*

Characteristics describe aspects of personality that tend to be true across genders, ages, ethnic groups, and cultures. A behavior is a specific expression of a characteristic and may be different from one person or group to another.

When we first begin to talk about type, we may describe preferences by naming behaviors we readily see in ourselves and in others. However, this tendency can lead to oversimplification. In the example of appropriate language, we identify the characteristic that people who have a Judging preference tend to be drawn to organization and planning. How people who prefer Judging accomplish that basic desire for organization and planning is an individual matter that results in observable behaviors. We avoid oversimplification when we describe the innate motivation rather than the observable, individualistic behavior.

The following example of Harry and his colleague illustrates the importance in communication of distinguishing characteristics from behavior.

Harry worked in a cultural exchange program between his college in the United States and a country in South America. He worked hard to adjust to the social manners of his colleagues, who spoke with great animation in what for him was uncomfortably close physical proximity. A colleague in the host country identified his own type as ISTJ. This type identity did not align with what Harry knew of ISTJ types. He assumed that only some Extraverts might be so animated in conversation and comfortable with such close physical contact. However, one characteristic of an ISTJ type is the tendency to be loyal to tradition. The colleague's behavior, then, was not an expression of Extraversion. Rather, it was motivated by loyalty to his particular tradition.

- **Use descriptors for a preference that are true for all types that include the preference.**

    Appropriate: People who have a preference for Thinking tend to use analysis in decision making. *(This statement reflects Thinking types.)*

    Inappropriate: People who have a preference for Thinking tend to analyze facts in decision making. *(This statement reflects only some Thinking types, those that pair Thinking with Sensing.)*

One way we oversimplify type is by describing a preference only in the way we ourselves use that preference. Eight of the sixteen types include any given preference. When we talk about type, we need to describe characteristics of a preference that fit for all eight types that include the preference.

Our tendency, however, is to describe characteristics that fit that preference only as the preference is expressed in our own type code. For example, a function is used differently depending upon which preferences are paired with it. People who have a preference for Sensing may use Thinking in a slightly different way than people who prefer Intuition and Thinking. In the inappropriate example just presented, we hear a description of Thinking that is true for the four types that include both Sensing and Thinking. People who prefer Sensing and Thinking are likely to use the Thinking function to analyze facts and data. However, four types pair Thinking with Intuition. People who prefer Intuition and Thinking are less likely to analyze data and facts and more likely to analyze concepts, ideas, or theoretical models. People of all eight types who have Thinking in their type code use analysis, but they do not all focus their use of analysis on the same things.

the art of dialogue

• Use type language rather than trait language.

One way we avoid oversimplification when we talk about type is to distinguish between type theories and trait theories, and to be aware of differences in language as we talk about each. One important characteristic of a type instrument is that it sorts into distinct categories. In contrast, a trait instrument measures the amount of a trait on a continuum. Type language describes alternatives or options, while trait language often uses comparison words such as *more* or *less*.

> **Sorting:** People who prefer Extraversion may prefer to communicate by talking, while those who prefer Introversion may prefer to communicate in writing.
>
> **Measuring:** People who prefer Extraversion tend to talk more than those who prefer Introversion.
>
> **Sorting:** I have a preference for Intuition.
>
> **Measuring:** I am more intuitive than my friend is.

When we begin to talk about type, we often use language that is appropriate for trait theories and instruments but is not appropriate for a type theory or instrument, such as the MBTI assessment tool. The tendency to use trait language is understandable. Many personality instruments are based on trait theories. Trait language permeates popular culture. As we have seen (page 80), the words *extraversion* and *introversion*, which Jung coined to name aspects of his psychological type theory, have entered common vocabulary and are regularly used as part of trait language.

The basic principles of type listed at the beginning of this chapter start with the statement that each type is valuable. Type language affirms that principle by describing each preference on a dichotomy in equally positive terms. In the first example of sorting language just presented, the description of Extraversion is equal in value to the description of Introversion. When we use words like *more* or *less* in a description as illustrated in the first example of measuring language, we risk the implication that one preference is better than the other.

In the second example of sorting language, a person has sorted between two alternatives on a dichotomy and named the one that is the person's preference. In the sentence identified as a measuring statement, two people are placed on a continuum. When we use statements that imply a continuum, we risk also implying that one end of the continuum is better than the other end. We affirm the basic but complex psychological constructs of type theory when we talk about type with sorting statements rather than measuring statements.

Upholding the Validity of Type Theory

Within the psychological field of assessing normal personality, the type theory developed by Jung, Briggs, and Myers and the MBTI instrument developed by Isabel Myers are noteworthy for the amount of research that supports the theory and instrument. In the technical terms of evaluating an instrument, the MBTI assessment tool has excellent reliability and validity. The value of the theory and instrument in any given situation, however, ultimately rests with the people who use the instrument and talk about type.

Any psychological theory or instrument has intended purposes and can be abused when it is used in ways that are contrary to the intended uses. In chapter 1, we saw that psychological type is not a way to pigeonhole, label, diagnose, prescribe, or excuse behavior, nor is it a description of everything about human behavior. Psychological type is an affirming way to understand ourselves and others and to recognize differences among people in typical, natural, and enduring patterns of preferences. Understanding the differences can benefit us in relationships and communication.

Some people will want to talk about type not only in their personal lives but also in work settings. They will see type theory and applications as a useful tool in their professions and will want to be able to administer and interpret the instrument. Those who are interested in becoming qualified users of type can find information about requirements and training for professional use through the publisher of the MBTI instrument, CPP, Inc., or through the publisher of this book, the Center for Applications of Psychological Type (CAPT).

Whether we talk about type personally or professionally, each of us plays a role in upholding the validity of type. We support the value of type when we use it for its intended purposes and talk about type as accurately as possible, doing our best to avoid stereotypes and oversimplification. We increase the likelihood that psychological type will be a valuable resource for us and for others when we are careful in how we talk about type.

the art of dialogue

chapter 15 **suggestions for further investigation of type and communication**

In this book, we have introduced a theory about the interaction of psychological type and communication. We have shown examples of type being expressed naturally in communication, adaptations of communication to type preferences, and some instances when communication is lacking. We have offered examples of out-of-pattern communication as well as examples of words that take on different meanings for different types.

The relationship between type and communication is an area with potential for more research. A few studies are cited in this book, and anecdotal examples are included, but the field of type and communication is wide open for further investigation.

Role of the Extraverted Function in Communication

Flavil Yeakley (1982, 1983, 1998) hypothesized that the primary communication channel for all types is the Extraverted function. He developed a formula to score ease or difficulty of communication, and he conducted research that appears to support the theory. Examples in part 3 of this book suggest that a speaker's first words are likely to be from the Extraverted function. Questions for further investigation on this theory include the following.

- If spoken language is recorded and analyzed, does evidence support the hypothesis that the Extraverted function is the primary communication channel?

- Are there particular circumstances in which the Extraverted function is not primary in communication? If so, what signals identify these circumstances?
- Are there situations when a person who introverts the dominant function speaks first from the dominant function rather than from the Extraverted function? If so, what defines such situations?

Out-of-Pattern Communication

Part 4 of this book offers examples of out-of-pattern communication. Naomi Quenk (2000, 2002) identifies stress, fatigue, use of alcohol or other mind-altering drugs, and illness as triggers for falling into the inferior function. Nancy Barger and Linda Kirby (1995) add that stress sometimes leads to exaggerated use of the dominant function. Lack of type development is considered by many type users to be a source of poor or inappropriate use of functions. This book suggests passion as a trigger for out-of-pattern communication. Questions for additional exploration include the following:

- What evidence is there for the concept of out-of-pattern communication?
- Do speech patterns change under particular circumstances? If so, what are those circumstances? What changes occur?
- Does a relationship exist between a specific trigger and which function is heard in oral communication?

Some examples in this book suggest that out-of-pattern speech disrupts dialogue. However, we must still ask the following questions:

- What is the evidence that communication is disrupted by out-of-pattern speech?
- Are there circumstances in which speech patterns change, but dialogue and communication continue?

Some type experts suggest, and experience supports, that a way to restore dialogue and communication when it is disrupted is to speak to a function on a dichotomy different from the one being used. Following this approach, a person in a communication event attempts to speak to the auxiliary or third function rather than to the dominant function when someone falls into the inferior function. (Note that the dominant function is the opposite of the inferior function.) For example, if a person speaks from an inferior function on the perception dichotomy (Sensing or Intuition), then he or she attempts to speak to the judgment dichotomy (Thinking or Feeling) since the dominant function will also be on the perception dichotomy. This area too can benefit from research on the following question:

- What are the results if type-alert speakers use an approach of speaking to a function on the opposite dichotomy as opposed to speaking to another function on the same dichotomy?

Listening

This book gives little attention to the role of functions in listening. The focus is on observations of functions in speaking. Marthanne Luzader (1995) investigated the hypothesis that a person speaks with the Extraverted function but listens with the Introverted function. Listening, then, is another area that offers opportunities for further research. Questions such as the following can be addressed.

- Do people use different functions for speaking and for listening? What is the evidence?

Yeakley (1983) suggests content to be attentive to when listening to speakers who prefer different functions. For example, he offers specific content to listen for when speakers prefer Sensing as opposed to Intuition. Yeakley also cautions listeners to avoid hearing more or different content than the speaker intends. The following questions offer opportunities for further investigation on this listening theory:

- What patterns of listening do listeners use when speakers say they have been heard?
- What are typical communication misunderstandings for each preference or type?

Word Analysis

Communication involves more than the use of language, but word analysis may be a fruitful area of investigation. Observations of type users have revealed that individuals use the same words and attribute different meanings to them. Type users also use different words to communicate the same meaning. Other examples come from the study of language patterns. Henry L. (Dick) Thompson (1995) has investigated the relationship between type preferences and definitions of words. Susan Brock (1991), in her studies of communication and type, found that different personality types use different words to convey the same meaning. Interesting questions to investigate further in this area include:

- What words have different meanings for different types? What are the differences in meaning?
- Do different types typically use different words to convey essentially the same meaning?

Other research has also been done on word analysis. Susan Brock (1994) and Larry Demarest (1997), among others, compiled words and phrases that people of each type frequently use. Researchers might ask:

- Are there specific words or phrases that people who have a particular preference or type typically use? Are there some they don't use?

A research project, which preceded publication of the fourth edition of *Introduction to Type* in 1987, identified words and phrases in type descriptions which people of the intended type agreed upon as descriptive of them and which communicated understanding of that type to other types. The following research question may be particularly relevant to those professionals who interpret MBTI® results:

- What words and phrases in interpretation language communicate understanding of psychological type to all types? To specific types?

Gender Differences

Gender differences in expression of preferences and types have long been of interest among type users. Answers to the following questions could bring important new understanding to this area:

- What does analysis of speech patterns show about males and females of the same type? What are the similarities? What are the differences?

Many applications of type exist, each with its own rich fields for investigation. Research in areas such as those suggested here can clarify how, when, and why type impacts what is said and what is heard. Such studies can deepen our understanding of the relationship between type and communication.

the art of dialogue

references and selected bibliography

Allen, Judy and Susan A. Brock. 2000. *Health care communication using personality type: Patients are different!* London: Routledge.

Barger, Nancy J. 1991. Workshop on type and communication. Newton KS.

Barger, Nancy J. and Linda K. Kirby. 1995. *The challenge of change in organizations.* Palo Alto CA: Davies-Black Publishing.

Brock, Susan A. 1991. *Flex Talk®.* Minneapolis MN: Brock Associates.

Brock, Susan A. 1994. *Using type in selling.* Palo Alto CA: CPP, Inc.

Demarest, Larry. 1997. *Looking at type in the workplace.* Gainesville FL: Center for Applications of Psychological Type.

DiTiberio, John K. and George H Jensen. 1995. *Writing and personality: Finding your voice, your style, your way.* Palo Alto CA: Davies-Black Publishing.

Edwards, Lloyd. 1993. *How we belong, fight, and pray.* Washington, DC: The Alban Institute.

Hirsh, Sandra K. and Jean M. Kummerow. 1998. *Introduction to type in organizations,* 3d ed. Palo Alto CA: CPP, Inc.

Kummerow, Jean M., Nancy J. Barger, and Linda K. Kirby. 1997. *WorkTypes.* New York NY: Warner Books, Inc.

Lawrence, Gordon. 1993. *People types and tiger stripes,* 3d ed. Gainesville FL: Center for Applications of Psychological Type.

Lawrence, Gordon and Charles Martin. 2001. *Building people, building programs: A practitioner's guide for introducing the MBTI to individuals and organizations.* Gainesville FL: Center for Applications of Psychological Type.

Luzader, Marthanne. 1995. Talking and listening with type. *Bulletin of Psychological Type,* 18: 3.

Martin, Charles. 1997. *Looking at type: The fundamentals.* Gainesville FL: Center for Applications of Psychological Type.

Murphy, Elizabeth. 1992. *The developing child.* Palo Alto CA: CPP, Inc.

Myers, Isabel Briggs. 1998. *Introduction to type,* 6th ed. Palo Alto CA: CPP, Inc.

Myers, Isabel Briggs and Mary H. McCaulley. 1985. *MBTI manual,* 2d ed. Palo Alto CA: CPP, Inc.

Myers, Isabel Briggs, Mary H. McCaulley, Naomi L. Quenk, and Allen L. Hammer. 1998. *MBTI manual,* 3d ed. Palo Alto CA: CPP, Inc.

Myers, Katharine D. and Linda K. Kirby. 1994. *Introduction to type dynamics and development: Exploring the next level of type.* Palo Alto CA: CPP, Inc.

Pearman, Roger R. and Sarah C. Albritton. 1997. *I'm not crazy, I'm just not you: The real meaning of the sixteen personality types.* Palo Alto CA: Davies-Black Publishing.

Penley, Janet P. and Diane W. Stephens. 1998. *The M.O.M.S.® handbook.* Wilmette IL: Penley and Associates, Inc.

Quenk, Naomi L. 2000. *In the grip: Understanding type, stress, and the inferior function,* 2d ed. Palo Alto CA: CPP, Inc.

Quenk, Naomi L. 2002. *Was that really me?* Palo Alto CA: Davies-Black Publishing.

Segal, Marci. 2003. *Quick guide to the four temperaments and creativity: A psychological understanding of innovation.* Huntington Beach CA: Telos Publications.

Thompson, Henry L. (Dick). 1995. *The CommunicationWheel™ workbook.* Watkinsville GA: High Performing Systems, Inc.

Tieger, Paul D. and Barbara Barron-Tieger. 2000. *Just your type.* Boston MA: Little, Brown & Company.

Yeakley, Flavil R., Jr. 1982. Communication style preferences and adjustments as an approach for studying effects of similarity in psychological type. *Research in Psychological Type, 5*: 30–48.

Yeakley, Flavil R., Jr. 1983. Implications of communication style research for psychological type theory. *Research in Psychological Type, 6*: 5–23.

Yeakley, Flavil R., Jr. 1998. Communicating with all types of people. Unpublished manuscript.

index*

A

adapt 5–6, 8, 23, 69, 74–75, 82, **88**, 160–161

affirmation 68

agendas for meetings 25

Allen, Judy 62, 173

alone and interaction time 22

appreciation 60

appropriate use 129

attitude 7, 50, 95, 97–99, 117–118, 126, 150, 157, 163, 173

auxiliary function 96–102, 103–104, 110, 125, 137–140, 149, 152–157, 161, 163

B

balance 94–98, 100-102, 145, 153–155

Barger, Nancy J. 8, 31, 134, 146, 151, 186

Barron-Tieger, Barbara 11, 66, 108

behavior similar, motivation different 32

bias 164, 178

body language 69

Briggs, Katharine Cook 4, 101–102, 145, 179–180, 184

Brock, Susan 22, 62, 74, 173, 187–188

C

characteristic 5, 32, 34, 35, 38, 51, 67, 79–80, 88, 94, 128, 136, 138, 148, 169, 179–182

clarifying thoughts 21

clues to preferences 48

constructive use of differences 4–5, 159, 161, 163–164

core 7, 27–28, 43, 55, 71, 94, 115

creativity **50**, 171–172

D

decision making 7, 27, 55, 67, 83, 95, 100, 131, 145, 149, 152, 153, 155, 156

Demarest, Larry 188

dichotomy 7, 13, 27, 48, 55, 97, 99, 122, 168, 180, 183

development of the third function 121

DiTiberio, John K. 35

differences are real 108

direction of energy 19

dominant function 96–101, 103-109, 118, 125, 136–138, 146–149, 150–152, 153–155, 163, 172-173

dynamics *See type dynamics*

E

Edwards, Lloyd 108

emotion 61–62, 108

emotions and Thinking types 62

exaggeration 133, 145-146, 148, 150–152, 153–157

Extraversion 6-7, 13–25, 80, 88, 94, 95–97, 100–102, 103, 106, 142, 159, 168–169, 170, 173, 180, 182, 183

Extraverted Feeling 106, 110–111, 125–126, 137, 149, 161, 162–163

Extraverted Intuition 116, 121, 127–129, 142, 148, 154–155, 157, 161

Extraverted Sensing 101, 117–118, 120–121, 124, 139-140, 173

Extraverted Thinking 106, 116, 122–124, 131, 137

F

Feeling 6, 7–8, 27, 55-70, 71, 73, 75, 78–79, 81-82, 83–84, 85-86, 87–89, 94, 95-101, 103, 106, 107–111, 115, 122, 124–125, 126–127, 146, 152, 153–155, 156, 159, 163, 167, 172, 174, 175, 180

fourth function 96, 98–99, 101, 104, 111, 129, 146–149, 163

> ***bold face = applications**

function 7, 43, 50, 55, 66, 71, 83–85, 94–102, 103-104, 115, 174

function pair 74, 78–79, 85, 88, 91

function the same, attitudes different 122

functions used one at a time 142

fundamental mental process 7, 43, 55, 95, 97, 100, 148

G

gender 65–66

getting unstuck 151

H

hierarchy of functions 94, 96, 101, 102, 115, 146, 148, 152, 178

Hirsh, Sandra K. 146

hypothesis 9, 10, 16, 46, 48, 74, 80, 98, 112, 121

I

inferior function 98-99, 146–151

falling into 148

information

definitions 47

gathering 7, 28, 43, 83, 95, 100, 131, 145, 148, 152, 153, 156

processing time 169

intelligence 52, 168, 171

Introversion 6–7, 13-25, 71, 80, 81, 88, 95-97, 100–102, 103, 109–111, 136, 142, 159, 168–169, 170, 173, 180, 183

Introverted Feeling 101, 111, 125–126, 129–132, 138–143, 161

Introverted Intuition 101, 121–122, 136–137, 151, 163

Introverted Sensing 109, 117–118, 129–131, 137–138, 161, 173

Introverted Thinking 122–124, 127–129, 157, 163

Intuition 6, 7–8, 28, 43–53, 71–73, 75, 78–79, 82, 83, 85-86, 88–89, 94–97, 99–101, 103, 111, 115, 122, 142, 146,

152, 153–154, 156, 159, 163, 168–169, 171–172, 174, 175

J

Jensen, George H. 35

Judging 6, 7–8, 27–40, 71, 88, 100, 101, 131, 159

judgment 7–8, 27–28, 55, 66, 83, 95–100, 102, 122, 142, 145, 149, 152, 153–155, 157

Jung, Carl G. 4, 80, 102, 145, 180, 183, 184

Kirby, Linda K. 8, 134, 146, 151, 186

Kummerow, Jean M. 8, 146

L

Lawrence, Gordon 12, 169, 177–178

lead function 95–97

leadership 82

least developed function 98

least preferred function 96, 98, 104

listening 4, 47, 59, 74, 83, 149, 165, 173–174

listening skills 59

Luzader, Marthanne 187

M

Martin, Charles 177–178

MBTI 4, 6, 51, 80, 85, 104, 109, 120, 180, 181, 183, 184

mode 8, 22–23, 87, 88, 133, 161

mode of communication 22

Murphy, Elizabeth 24, 38, 68

Murphy-Meisgeier Type Indicator for Children 86

Myers, Isabel Briggs 2, 4, 101–102, 145, 159, 163, 178–180, 184

Myers-Briggs Type Indicator See MBTI

N

NT and communication 86

O

occupational choices **64**

oral and written communication **17**

orientation **7, 27–28, 50, 71**

P

parenting a child with an Extraversion or Introversion preference **24**

parenting a child with a Judging or Perceiving preference **38**

passion 135–140

Penley, Janet P. 66

Perceiving 6, 7–8, 27–40, 71, 88, 100, 102, 154, 159, 172

perception 7–8, 28, 43, 55, 66, 83, 95–100, 102, 142, 145, 148–149, 152, 153, 155, 157

personal lives **70**

personality type 9, 11, 66, 69, 74, 95, 96, 146

precise words **80**

preference 5–7, 13, 17–20, 22–24, 27–28, 31–36, 38–40, 43, 46–51, 55, 58–60, 62, 64–70, 71–74, 79–83, 85–88, 91, 93–94, 95–97, 100, 107–111, 115, 117–118, 121–122, 124–127, 131, 136, 142, 156, 159, 163–164, 178–183

primary communication function 103–104, 110–111, 136–137, 140, 142, 161, 163

procrastination **34**, 99

psychological type 4–9, 10, 11, 17, 22, 23, 27, 32, 43, 55, 71, 74, 80, 83, 91, 93, 95–96, 113, 115, 145, 154, 162, 177, 180, 181, 183, 184, 185

Q

Quenk, Naomi L. 146, 186

R

reality and imagination 51

recharging the Introversion battery 21

S

secondary communication function 104, 140

Segal, Marci 171

Sensing 6, 7–8, 28, 43–53, 71–73, 74, 78–79, 82, 83, 85–86, 88–89, 94–97, 99–101, 103, 107, 111, 115, 122, 125, 142, 146, 151–152, 153, 156, 159, 161, 163, 168-169, 171–174

speaking to both Sensing and Intuitive types **49**

Stephens, Diane W. 66

stereotype 177–180

stress 3, 34, 38, 83, 99, 139, 140, 142, 145–151

supporting function 95, 97

T

teaching to Sensing and Intuitive preferences **52**

tension source **126**

tertiary function 96–97, 101

Thinking 6, 7–8, 27, 55–70, 71, 73, 74, 79–80, 81–82, 83, 85–86, 87–89, 94–101, 103, 106, 107, 109, 115, 125, 129, 142, 146, 153–154, 156, 159, 167, 172, 174, 175, 182

third function 96–99, 101, 104, 121, 124–125, 129, 147–150

Thompson, Henry L. (Dick) 187

Tieger, Paul D. 11, 66, 108

trait 183

type code 7, 13, 16, 27, 43, 55, 74, 91, 93–97, 100–101, 120–121, 182

type development 23, 85, 97, 99, 121, **124**–125, 145, 147, 152–157

process **156**

type dynamics 91, 92–102, 103–107, 109–111, 115, 120–121, 122, 124, 128–129, 130–131, 136–137, 139, 141, 148–149, 151–152, 153–154, 159, 162–164

type is not an excuse **81**

type language 8, 27, 178, 181, 183

typical patterns **18**

U

undeveloped preferences 154
unheard functions 131

V

validity 184
verification 5, 9, 86

W

writing starters 35

Y

Yeakley, Flavil R. 103, 109–110, 112–113,
    166, 174, 185, 187

Z

Z pattern 83–85

resources

If you do not know your psychological type preferences and would like to learn about them by taking the Myers-Briggs Type Indicator® instrument, go to Take the MBTI® Assessment on the CAPT Web site, www.capt.org. You can also contact the Scoring Department at 800.777.CAPT, ext. 104.

To learn more about the Myers-Briggs Type Indicator instrument, to purchase books and multimedia materials related to the MBTI, or to enroll in training classes in the applications and use of the Indicator, please contact the Center for Applications of Psychological Type. Or visit the Web site for a complete listing of training classes and products.

The Center for Applications of Psychological Type (CAPT)
2815 NW 13th Street, Suite 401
Gainesville FL 32609

800.777.2278 (toll-free USA and Canada)
352.375.0160

www.capt.org

Also from the Center for Applications of Psychological Type

LOOKING AT TYPE®: THE FUNDAMENTALS
Charles R. Martin

Looking at Type®: The Fundamentals is designed to give the person who has just discovered type a more comprehensive picture of their MBTI results than is provided by the basic scoring process. Learning about the many applications of type can enrich relationships, aid decision-making, and increase a sense of self-worth and personal competence. Each of the 16 type descriptions indicates unique paths to personal growth and achievement. The narrative includes the role of type in relationships, communication, and problem solving. Perfect for MBTI trainers to hand out at workshops or for individuals wanting to better understand their own psychological type preferences.

▸ Book, paperback. 60 pages. CAPT. 1997. Product No. 60107.
▸ Product No. 60122.A. (package of 10).
▸ Spanish Version. Product No. 60148.
▸ Spanish Version. Product No. 60119.A (package of 10).

WIRED FOR CONFLICT
Sondra S. VanSant

Wired for Conflict by well-known educator and psychological type expert Sondra VanSant is an excellent book for learning how to manage conflict . . . both at home and in the workplace. By understanding the innate differences between the people we know . . . and sometimes love . . . conflict can be diffused before it begins. This book is a great teaching tool for those new to the concepts of psychological type. It also serves to guide the consultant who addresses conflict in their professional practice.

The structure provides:
  ▸ Practical examples
  ▸ Tips for all MBTI types
  ▸ Easy-to-follow charts
  ▸ Step-by-step methods for implementing conflict resolution

▸ Book, paperback. 105 pages. CAPT. 2003. Product No. 60191.

PEOPLE TYPES & TIGER STRIPES
Gordon D. Lawrence

People Types & Tiger Stripes is a classic general book on the use and application of the MBTI instrument as well as the definitive book in the field of education and type. This edition reflects the author's extensive work and expertise in the field of psychological type. *People Types & Tiger Stripes* also includes two writings by Isabel Briggs Myers. Third edition.

▸ Book, paperback. 243 pages. CAPT. 1993. Product No. 60002.